THE CHINESE
MARTIAL CODE

THE CHINESE MARTIAL CODE

THE ART OF WAR OF SUN TZU
THE PRECEPTS OF WAR BY SIMA RANGJU
WU ZI ON THE ART OF WAR

BILINGUAL EDITION
Annotated English translations with complete Chinese texts

Translations by **Arthur Lindsay Sadler**
Foreword and annotations by **Edwin Lowe**

TUTTLE PUBLISHING
Tokyo • Rutland, Vermont • Singapore

Published by Tuttle Publishing, an imprint of Periplus Editions (HK) Ltd., with editorial offices at 364 Innovation Drive, North Clarendon, Vermont 05759 U.S.A.

Foreword and Annotations Copyright © 2009 Periplus Editions (HK) Ltd.

Library of Congress Cataloging-in-Publication Data

Three military classics of China.
   The Chinese martial code / [translated and with commentary] by Arthur Lindsay Sadler; foreword and annotations by Edwin Lowe.
       p. cm.
   Originally published: Sydney: Australasian Medical Pub. Co., 1944, under title Three military classics of China.
   Includes bibliographical references.
   ISBN 978-0-8048-4004-0 (pbk.)
1. Military art and science—China—Early works to 1800. 2. Sunzi, 6th cent. B. C. Sunzi bing fa. 3. Sima, Ranju, 4th cent. B.C. Sima fa. 4. Wu, Qi, 440-381 B.C. Wuzi. I. Sadler, A. L. (Arthur Lindsay), b. 1882. II. Lowe, Edwin, 1972-III. Sunzi B.C. Wuzi. VI. Title.
   U43.C6T47 2008
   355.02—dc22

                                           2008047138

ISBN 978-0-8048-4004-0

Distributed by
North America, Latin America & Europe
Tuttle Publishing
364 Innovation Drive
North Clarendon, VT 05759-9436 U.S.A.
Tel: 1 (802) 773-8930; Fax: 1 (802) 773-6993
info@tuttlepublishing.com
www.tuttlepublishing.com

Japan
Tuttle Publishing
Yaekari Building, 3rd Floor
5-4-12 Osaki
Shinagawa-ku
Tokyo 141 0032
Tel: (81) 3 5437-0171; Fax: (81) 3 5437-0755
tuttle-sales@gol.com

Asia Pacific
Berkeley Books Pte. Ltd.
61 Tai Seng Avenue #02-12
Singapore 534167
Tel: (65) 6280-1330
Fax: (65) 6280-6290
inquiries@periplus.com.sg
www.periplus.com

13 12 11 10 09   10 9 8 7 6 5 4 3 2 1

Printed in the United States

TUTTLE PUBLISHING® is a registered trademark of Tuttle Publishing, a division of Periplus Editions (HK) Ltd.

Table of Contents

For my father Henry who loved the classics,

and

For Emma, who taught me to better love both.

Preface

About The Book, Translation, and Romanization

THE *Chinese Martial Code* was originally published as *Three Military Classics of China* by Professor A.L. Sadler, The University of Sydney by the Australasian Medical Publishing Co. Ltd., Sydney 1944.

This edition, *The Chinese Martial Code* marks the first reprint of this pioneering work in the translation of classic Chinese strategic texts and of Arthur L. Sadler's brief, but pioneering commentary in what is today described as "strategic culture."

The intention of this second and revised edition of Arthur Sadler's translations is to present his pioneering but little circulated work to a new audience, preserving as much as possible, the form in which he originally presented them. Accordingly, this edition of Sadler's translation is updated only in the romanisation of Chinese words and names. An eminent Japanologist, Arthur Sadler translated these texts from the original Chinese classics. In doing so, Sadler used the then standard system of romanisation of Chinese names and places, the Wade-Giles system. In this revision, I have used the modern *pinyin* system of romanisation which is the official standard of the People's Republic of China. While neither system renders correct pronunciation of Chinese clear or easy for the general English speaking reader, I have chosen to use the *pinyin* system due to its official status and its almost universal use in the teaching of the Chinese language both within China and internationally. There remains a degree of recalcitrance in the adherence to the Wade-Giles system in popular publishing and even in scholarship. However for those students of the Chinese language

taught according to the official standards of the Office of the
Chinese Language Council of the People's Republic of China,
pinyin will be the familiar system.

In the process of romanisation of Chinese names and words
to *pinyin*, I have referred to the original Chinese language
texts in and rendered the Chinese characters directly into the
pinyin system. The only and most prominent exception to the
romanisation system is in the name of Sun Tzu or "Master
Sun," which I have retained in the former Wade-Giles system.
My editor informs me that most readers will be familiar with
"Sun Tzu", rather than the *pinyin* version of "Sun Zi," so I
have deferred to his experience and judgement. There is a long
established scholarly precedence for this, in the near universal
use of the Latin appellations of Confucius and Mencius rather
than their Chinese versions of Kong Zi and Meng Zi. To those
readers who prefer "Sun Tzu" to "Sun Zi," let me take the opportunity to remind you that "Tzu" is not read with the "u"
sound. "Tzu" is pronounced as "Zi." To my fellow purist and
pedants, I do apologise.

In Arthur Sadler's original 1944 translation of the texts into
English, there are some passages which seem either awkward
or even incorrect in the wider context, when read either in the
original Chinese or in more recent scholarly translations. I have
considered the possible reasons for these problems in my own
introductory notes. However, I have elected to retain Sadler's
original translations for the sake of continuity and because often, they remain eminently readable for the non-Sinologist and
general reader. Wherever I believe that clarification or a correction of Sadler's translation is warranted, I have included it
as a footnote.*

---

* Chinese reference texts are: Roger Ames, *Sun Tzu The Art of Warfare. The First
English Translation Incorporating the Yin-Ch' ueh-Shan Texts. Translated with an Introduction and Commentary by Roger T. Ames.* (Ballantine Books, NY 1993);

Liu Zhongping, "*Sima fa jin zhu jin yi. Liu Zhongping zhu yi ; Zhonghua wen hua fu
xing yun dong tui xing wei yuan hui, Guo li bian yi guan Zhonghua cong shu bian shen
wei yuan hui.*" (*Sima Fa with Modern Commentary.* Commentary by Liu Zhongping.
Editor in Chief, Committee for the Advancement of the Revival of Chinese Culture. Edi-

The Chinese titles of the three classical texts in Sadler's book are themselves subject of some difficulty in translation, due to the vagaries of the classical Chinese language, and in part due to established conventions in English translation. The process behind the translation of the titles in the first and second editions of Sadler's work illustrates some of that difficulty. The original Chinese titles, along with their "correct" philological translations into English are *Sun Zi Bingfa* ("Master Sun's Art of Warfare"), *Sima Fa* ("The Methods of the Minister of War") and *Wu Zi* ("Master Wu"). These were translated by Sadler in his 1944 edition as *The Articles of Sun Tz', The Precepts of Ssu Ma Jang Chu* and *Wu Chi on the Art of War.* In seeking the balance between scholarly accuracy, academic and literary convention, and literary continuity, these texts have been titled in this edition as: *The Art of War of Sun Tzu, The Precepts of War by Sima Rangju* and *Wu Zi on the Art of War.* In the interest of brevity, I have in places referred to the classic texts according to the convention used in Chinese studies; *Sun Tzu, Sima Fa* and *Wu Zi.* When I have referred to the person, I have mostly use their personal names, Sun Wu, Sima Rangju and Wu Qi to prevent confusion. In a few places, the use of their titles of "Sun Tzu," "Wu Zi," or "Sima" has been warranted.

I have not undertaken any extensive scholarship on the texts, as this has been done comprehensively by other scholars. I have referred to some of these in both English and Chinese (for the benefit of those with Chinese language skills) where necessary. In this edition, I have provided a basic biography and overview of works of the three strategic writers, Sun Tzu, Sima Rangju, and Wu Qi. Additionally, I have made further

tor in Chief, of the Committee of the Chinese Collection, National Translation Service. Revised Edition. Taipei, Taiwan Commercial Press 1986);

Fu Shaojie, *Wuzi jin zhu jin yi. Fu Shaojie zhu yi; Zhonghua wen hua fu xing yun dong tui xing wei yuan hui, Guo li bian yi guan Zhonghua cong shu bian shen wei yuan hui. Xiu ding chu ban. Publisher: Taibei shi : Taiwan shang wu yin shu guan, (Wu Zi with Modern Commentary.* Commentary by Fu Shaojie. Editor in Chief, Committee for the Advancement of the Revival of Chinese Culture. Editor in Chief, of the Committee of the Chinese Collection, National Translation Service. Revised Edition. Taipei, Taiwan Commercial Press 1985).

additional introductory comments or annotations to the classic texts in areas of current scholarship in Chinese strategic studies or to episodes in history wherever I have considered them appropriate.

In this edition, I have included biographical information of Professor Arthur L. Sadler and his scholarship in East Asian studies. This includes his pioneering work in the translation of classic Chinese strategic texts and his pioneering commentary on strategic culture. I have also discussed the importance of cultural understanding and strategic culture in strategic and security studies in the 21st Century.

In the completion of this book, as with everything else, I must thank Emma Runcie for her love and unconditional support. My gratitude goes to Tuttle Publishing and my editor, William Notte for allowing me the opportunity to discover and present the pioneering work of Professor Arthur L. Sadler. At Macquarie University, Sydney, my thanks go to Dr. Shirley Chan and to Professor Daniel Kane. I am glad to know that my modest ability in reading, translation, and interpretation of classical Chinese does actually show some coherence and cogency.

My greatest appreciation goes to Lieutenant Commander Marsden C. Hordern VRD, BA, Hon DLitt (*Syd*), RANR (retd); infantryman, gunner, World War II Patrol Boat Man and scholar. Your generous hospitality at "Rivenhall," your personal insight to Professor Sadler, and your knowledge of things learned as a young man helped bring the great Professor back to life so that I might "get inside his head" and see the world through his eyes. We can only aspire to his brilliance.

Edwin H. Lowe
Macquarie University
Sydney 2008

Foreword

In 1944, at the height of Australia's war against Japan in the South West Pacific, the eminent Japanologist Arthur Lindsay Sadler, Professor of Oriental Studies at The University of Sydney and one time Professor of Japanese of the Royal Military College of Australia, published his translations of three classics of strategic thought and statecraft of ancient China.

The *Three Military Classics of China* was an unassuming work which seemed to have been little circulated in its time. However, it was a remarkable work, given the nature of the texts, the period in which it was written, and the intent in which Sadler intended it to be read and understood.* Under the constraints of the war in the South West Pacific, with his former students fighting the Japanese forces in New Guinea, Sadler hurriedly translated the classical strategic texts of *Sun Zi Bingfa* (*Sun Tzu's The Art of War*), *Sima Fa* (*The Methods of The Minister of War*), and *Wu Zi* (*Wu Zi on the Art of War*). Despite the limited circulation, the pressure of wartime scholarship and publishing, and perhaps despite Sadler's unassuming nature, the publication of this book was a landmark, not only in the translation of classic Chinese texts, but more importantly, in the nascent fields of Chinese strategic studies and strategic culture.

Far from being forgotten and obscure writings limited to a small intellectual or professional elite, the texts translated by Sadler, *The Art of War of Sun Tzu, The Precepts of War of Sima Rangju,* and *Wu Qi on the Art of War*, along with other canoni-

---

* A. L. Sadler, *Three Military Classics of China*. Australasian Medical Publishing Company Ltd, Sydney 1944.

cal texts, have been an enduring literary tradition in China and East Asia for over 2000 years.

Originally complied during the social and political chaos of the Spring and Autumn Period (722-481 BCE) and amended and edited through this time and into the Warring States Period (ca 403–221 BCE), these texts are more than simple military field manuals of bronze and iron age China. Rooted deeply in the formative traditions of Chinese socio-political thought, this literary corpus represents the fundamental principles of Chinese strategic thought and statecraft that have shaped the strategic culture and political landscape of East Asia for over two millennia.

These three classic texts, along with other contemporary Spring and Autumn and Warring States texts, were transmitted in the canonical tradition for over a thousand years. During the Song Dynasty (970 -1279 CE), the surviving classical texts of strategy and statecraft from antiquity were collected and edited into a compilation known as the *Seven Military Classics*.

Most well known of all Chinese strategic texts, is of course *The Art of War of Sun Tzu*, the oldest of the entire classic strategic corpus. More than a professional guide for soldiers and statesmen, *Sun Tzu* has been an essential part of the East Asian literary tradition, where it has remained a vibrant living tradition over the centuries through both the scholarship and the strategic skills of scholar-soldiers such as Cao Cao, Mao Zedong and Võ Nguyên Giáp. In more recent times this tradition has continued on a mass scale through popular culture, such as novels and latterly, paperbacks, comic books, and computer games. Through the use of written Chinese as the *lingua franca* of literary culture throughout East Asia, the tradition of Chinese strategic thought is as much a deep and enduring intellectual tradition in Vietnam, Japan, and Korea as it is in China. The precepts and dimensions of Chinese strategic thought (and of *Sun Tzu* in particular) form an essential part of the wider East Asian consciousness, not only in military and political affairs, but equally so in human relations, sports, games, business, and corporate affairs.

Chinese Strategic Thought

The tradition of strategic and military thought in the Chinese world has its origins in the classical age of the foundation of Chinese philosophy. Sharing a common heritage with Confucianism, Legalism, Daoism, and others of the "Hundred Schools of Thought," Chinese strategic texts share the distinction of being among the most widely read and studied classics of humanity. Chinese strategic thought shares the same wider elements of the "traditional" forms of philosophy, since they were all devised as responses to the same sociological and political problems of the era. The schools of classical Chinese thought are almost all of *applied philosophy* in nature. Classical strategic thought is no exception–almost all of the classical strategists contemplated the practical problems of statecraft and warfare through sustained philosophical reflection.* Similarly, though it is not commonly noted, many of the other core Chinese philosophic texts such as *The Book of Lord Shang*, Confucius' *The Analects, Mencius, Han Fei Zi* and the *Daodejing* contain either lengthy commentary or extended statements on military thought.† Conversely, those texts normally considered "strategic" or "military" texts, including *Sun Tzu, Sima Fa*, and *Wu Zi* contain extended discussion on the government of civil society and the nature of civil order. Indeed Han Fei Zi (ca 280–233 BCE) himself noted that discussions on strategy were popular among scholars and that many of them possessed copies of *Sun Tzu* and *Wu Zi*.‡ For those of us living in the present day, and in a culture so different to that of classical China's, an understanding of the nature of Chinese strategic thought requires an understanding of this holistic or unifying nature of classical Chinese thought itself. Furthermore, in order for us to

---

* Roger Ames, *Sun Tzu The Art of Warfare. The First English Translation Incorporating the Yin-Ch"ueh-Shan Texts. Translated with an Introduction and Commentary by Roger T. Ames.* (Ballantine Books, NY 1993). p7.

† *Ibid.*

‡ Alistair Iain Johnston, *Cultural Realism. Strategic Culture and Grand Strategy in Chinese History.* (Princeton University Press, Princeton. 1995). p41.

understand the classic strategic texts in their proper contexts, it is critical to understand the broader intellectual environment and the historical landscape of the time.

At the time of the Warring States Period (ca 403–221 BCE), China was in a state of social and political chaos. The social and political order which had been established by the Zhou Dynasty (beginning ca 1027 BCE) was in its decline. The early period, or the Western Zhou Dynasty, at the height of the Chinese Bronze Age was considered, even at the time of the Warring States as the great period of antiquity and the zenith of Chinese civilization. During the Western Zhou, the foundations of Chinese cosmology and philosophy, as well as the great creation myths of Chinese culture had developed and had coalesced into a literary and historical narrative. The earliest literary records, such as *The Book of Changes*, *The Book of Songs,* and *The Book of History*, formed the basis not only of China's literary culture, but the very founding tenets of Chinese civilization itself.*

The political system of the Western Zhou, based on the central rule of the Zhou Kings over fiefdoms, was by the time of the Spring and Autumn Period (722–481 BCE) of the latter or Eastern Zhou Dynasty, in ruins. The decline of the Eastern Zhou Dynasty (722–221 BCE) is marked as a period of over five hundred years of continual feudal warfare and social unrest.

At the height of the Western Zhou Dynasty, the Zhou Kings claimed the ritual homage over 1800 fiefdoms.† However, with the decline of central power in the Zhou state and corresponding rise of feudal power and regional cultural identities, the political climate became increasingly fractious and contentious as feudal lords vied for power over one another.‡ By the time of the start of the Eastern Zhou (771 BCE), the power and authority of the Zhou Kings had been reduced to a nominal and

---

* Also known as the *I Ching, Book of Poetry* and *Book of Documents* respectively.

† Bai Shouyi, *An Outline History of China,* (Foreign Languages Press, Beijing. 1982), p89.

‡ Ralph D. Sawyer, *The Seven Military Classics of Ancient China (Wu Jing Qi Shu)* translation and commentary by Ralph D. Sawyer, with Mei-chün Sawyer. (Westview Press, Boulder 1993), p8

ceremonial role, as the exercise real power devolved into the hands of the hereditary feudal lords. The Zhou King and the capital itself became dependent on the support of the most powerful fiefdoms, which had by the time of the beginning of the Spring and Autumn Period (722 BCE) been reduced to 100 fiefdoms after years of internecine struggle.* Over the course of the Spring and Autumn Period, these fiefdoms became increasingly independent of the Zhou court, as generational shifts weakened the original feudal ties of ceremonial ritual and clan kinship. Correspondingly, as the *de jure* authority of the Zhou Kings weakened, the balance of power shifted from the center to the periphery, as the feudal lords established *de facto* independent states. These semiautonomous polities contended with each other for hegemonic power with an ever increasing level of sophistication and complexity in political maneuver and in the levels of military force and violence.

As the latter part of the Eastern Zhou descended into the period known as the Warring States (403–221 BCE), the Zhou state had fragmented into seven kingdoms. Ruled by self declared Kings and thus effectively ending the *de jure* Zhou suzerainty, the states contended for hegemony. By the end of this period, Chinese civilization had been transformed into one of the bloodiest epochs in history, ending only in the military reunification by the state of Qin and the foundation of the First Empire of Qin (221 BCE).

During the Spring and Autumn Period, warfare had been transformed from an aristocratic pursuit, complete with rituals and chivalry, into a "fundamental occupation" and a national industry of anonymous large scale engagements, backed by the total resources of state.† This "revolution in military affairs" of harnessing the power of the people, the army, and the government, pre-empted the first Western experience in Napoleonic France, described by Carl von Clausewitz as the "remarkable

---

* Bai *Op.cit.*

† See also Ames (1993) p4; and Sawyer (1993) pp9-11.

trinity" by more than two thousand years.* Similarly, the modern concept of "total war" as understood by the modern strategist, was waged in China a full two thousand years before Napoleon Bonaparte's *Grande Armée* created by the *levée en masse* and William Tecumseh Sherman's total war strategy of "hard war."† By the Warring States period, states fielded enormous conscript armies as large as the combined armies of the Roman Empire and for logistical support, civilian populations were mobilised on a scale unseen in the West until the Great War.‡ These armies were commanded by a professional cadre of officers, often gifted representatives of the lower classes of society and using the latest in military technology, such as native Chinese cavalry, bronze-chromium alloy and iron swords, weapon heads, and crossbows. Deceit, fraud, and bribery became the mainstay of diplomacy and espionage flourished and became an art form.§ As the casualties on the field climbed into the hundreds of thousands in each engagement, it became apparent that the stakes in warfare had been raised to the ultimate level—that to lose in war would result in national destruction.

Mirroring external relations, internal socio-political conditions were in turmoil as the social order disintegrated. Many of the houses from the old aristocracy from the Zhou clan

---

* Carl von Clausewitz, *On War,* translated by Michael Howard and Peter Paret. (Princeton University Press, Princeton. 1984), p89.

† Bonaparte and Sherman may be considered as the first of the "modern generals" of the industrial age in the West. Napoleon Bonaparte pioneered the creation of a national conscript army, the *Grande Armée* during the Napoleonic Wars (1803-1815) with the earlier revolutionary decree of the *levée en masse* which was intended to direct the resources of the civil population into a war effort. During the American Civil War (1861-1865) William T. Sherman pioneered the concept of waging war against the material and economic power of an enemy state. During Sherman's "March to the Sea" of the Georgia campaign of 1864, Sherman explicitly waged a modern total war strategy of destruction of enemy economic and material infrastructure in order to destroy his ability to make war. This strategy, endorsed as by the US government and army, was later continued in Sherman's Carolinas campaign in 1865.

‡ Christopher Coker, "What Would Sun Tzu Say about The War on Terrorism?" *RUSI Journal*, (Royal United Services Institute for Defence and Security Studies, London) Feb 2003, Vol. 148, No. 1.

§ Samuel B. Griffith, *Sun Tzu The Art of War. Translated and with an Introduction by Samuel B. Griffith, with a forward by B.H. Liddle Hart.* (Oxford University Press, Oxford 1963), p24.

declined and new houses rose through conquest or internal ascendance. As the internal centers of power shifted, new classes of gifted lower aristocracy, government officials, generals, and others of humble origin, rose to prominence with talent, as the old social order fell.* The civilised and ritual forms of aristocratic behaviour of the Zhou system fell into disuse as treason and corruption became the norm amongst the new classes of socially mobile generals and ministers. Education and literacy declined and Confucius, the Great Sage himself, complained bitterly about the fall in standards of literacy and language.† Civil society fell into frightening depths of brutality as crimes became punishable by death and severe forms of mutilation in an attempt to bring order to the chaos.‡

During the early Spring and Autumn Period, both civil and military affairs remained the realm of the aristocracy as had been the case in the early Zhou period. Members of the ruling houses were trained from an early age in the arts of warfare and government, and even Confucius, whose thoughts were concerned with the nature of humanity and social order, was clearly trained for both a literary and military career.§ However by the time of the Warring States Period, the business of state itself rose to new heights of complexity and professionalism, as the civil and military professions diverged. Just as the military sphere grew in size and complexity in response to the escalation of conflict, so too did the civil spheres of population, commerce, agriculture, and industry. Accordingly, the successful management of state affairs, upon which the survival of the state itself ultimately depended, demanded an increasing sophistication in expertise of its rulers and ministers. Most states

---

* Edwin H. Lowe, *Transcending the Cultural Gaps in 21st Century Strategic Analysis and Planning: the Real Revolution in Military Affairs*. Canberra Papers on Strategy and Defence No.155, (Strategic and Defence Studies Center, Australian National University 2004). p16.

† Confucius's conversation with Zilu on "the rectification of names" in *The Analects* XIII.3. See D.C. Lau, *Confucius. The Analects*. (Penguin Books, London 1979), p118.

‡ Griffith (1963), p23.

§ Ames (1993), p41.

held the entire male population liable for military service, with the Qin state (which eventually unified the empire by force) going as far as organising the whole of civil society into administrative structures that enabled rapid mass mobilization along the pre-prepared lines.*

It was against this tumultuous backdrop of military-civil disorder and the need for professional expertise in government and statecraft that the roots of Chinese cultural traditions, practices, and philosophies were laid down. Amidst the political and social turmoil of the Spring and Autumn Period and the Warring States, scholars, philosophers, and experts in military and civil affairs gained a critical importance in intellectual and socio-political life. Carrying with them their ideas of social and military theories, hundreds of these itinerant philosophers wandered from state to state seeking patronage of the courts and an opportunity to implement their philosophies. Some like Confucius, Zhuang Zi, Xun Zi, and Gao Zi sought to stop the carnage by restoring social order through social rectification. Others, more realist philosophers such as Sun Tzu and Wu Zi sought national survival in a world of constant war. Accordingly, in almost all of the competing schools of thought of this era, the emphasis lay not in the metaphysical and spiritual realms, but in the very pragmatic realms of practical statecraft.

Among these "Hundred Schools of Thought" were the Mohist, the Legalists, and the Logicians, each of whom were to achieve varying levels of success in implementing their concepts on the various states.† The Mohist formed a quasi-spiritual military order of philosophers advocating "universal love" and expert in defensive siege warfare and springing to the assistance of states under attack. The Legalist achieved prominence in the state of Qin and later in the unified Qin Empire, by implement-

---

* Sawyer (1993) p375. This was later emulated in the 1960s by the organisation of the People's Militia along the lines of the civil structure of rural communes.

† The Legalists were derived from a branch of Confucianism, later considered as heterodoxy. For more detail on the Hundred Schools of Thought, see Conrad Schirokauer, *A Brief History of Chinese Civilization* (Harcourt Brace and Co., Orlando, 1991).

ing an absolutist system of rule of law, complemented by an un-compromising and brutal system of punishment. Philosophies that bore little relevance or did not offer practical solutions to the pressing socio-political problems of the era, such as those of the Logicians, did not gain much traction.* However, of these many schools of thought, it was to be the Confucians and the Daoists who, together, were to stamp an indelible influence onto Chinese civilization and Chinese strategic thought.

The Confucians were concerned primarily with the role of human values in the nature of government and social order amidst the social and political turmoil. Born during the Spring and Autumn Period, Confucius (551–479 BCE) turned towards the example of the "golden age" of the early Zhou Dynasty, teaching that universal order was dependent on the proper relationships between men. Confucius believed that the proper rites of propriety and sincerity must govern the relationship between men and that, individually, man must act with virtue and strive for righteousness and benevolence in his actions. Rather than a model of individual human behaviour, Confucius set this firmly in the context of the five cardinal relationships of society: father and son, ruler and minister, husband and wife, elder and younger brother, friend and friend. The proper behaviour within these relationships was determined by the reciprocal obligations between individuals and their hierarchical status. The Confucians believed that when men observed and practised the correct human behaviours across the range of human and social relationships, the intrinsic diffusive interrelatedness of society and humanity would set the inner self, the family, the state, and the universe in harmony and order. Rulers, ministers and governments, mirroring individual virtue, would act with

---

* The philosophy of the Logicians is the school of thought that most is most comparable with that of the classical Greek philosophers. With little following at any time given its lack of practicality to the problems of the day, the philosophy of logical thought made little subsequent impact on Chinese thought and cultural paradigms. The Legalist tradition was derived from the school thought advocated by the Confucian scholar Xun Zi, therefore it is considered a heterodox form of Confucianism, but Confucian in origin none the less.

benevolence, righteousness, and ritual propriety, thus creating harmony within the state and in diplomatic relations.

Confucianism, with its hierarchical rigidity and ideals of human behaviour has provided the model for government and social order in the Chinese world. However, quite conversely, it has been Daoism with its ambiguity that has defined the Chinese world view and natural order. Attributed to the legendary figure Lao Zi during the Spring and Autumn Period, the *Daodejing (The Classic of the Dao)* emphasised the attainment of universal order by the return of humanity to harmony with the natural order. It advocated an understanding of primal simplicity and of the natural order of the world, which would result in the attainment of social and political order. Daoism's philosophies have shaped the Chinese world view, with its abstract, paradoxical and cryptic concepts of humanity and the natural order. The influence of Daoism is so pervasive that it continues to influence almost every aspect of Chinese civilization and its influence can be found in Chinese medicine and scientific thought, spirituality, literature, aesthetics, architecture, martial arts, and, of course politics, grand strategy, and warfare.*

Central to this natural order, is the *Dao*.† The concept of the *Dao* defies not only translation, but at its very essence, defies definition. Indeed, the ambiguity of the concept is emphasised in the very first phrase of the *Daodejing*: "The *Dao* that can be spoken, is not the true *Dao*. The Name that can be Named, is not the true name."‡ However the need to define that *Dao* in order to examine it, leads us to loosely translate it as "the Way," "the method," "the path," "the road," or "the name," and so on, depending on the context that it is being used.§ It is the uni-

---

* Thomas Cleary *The Inner Teachings of Taoism* Chang Po-tuan, commentary by Liu I-ming, translated by Thomas Cleary. (Shambala, Boston 1986). p.vii.

† Or *Tao* (Wade-Giles). The *Dao* may also be familiar by its form as "*Do*" as in *kendo* (the Way of the sword) and *bushido* ("the Way of the warrior").

‡ After D.C. Lau, *Lao Tzu Tao Te Ching. Translated with an Introduction by D.C. Lau*, Penguin, (London 1963). I.1.

§ The word *Dao* is also used in other contemporary schools of thought such as Confucianism, and it may be translated in the same manner. What differs is the constitutive or formative aspects of "the Way" in a particular school of thought.

versal principal of all things, the one way.* Even so, the *Dao* can
not be so strictly defined, for its very nature is highly abstract
and contextual. The *Dao* can not be known or understood
through scientific rationalism or metaphysical objectivism. The
Dao can only be "realised," "intuited," or "distilled" through
contextualising the nature of its constituent and interrelated
parts, and by *comprehensively* contemplating and intuiting the
ever changing dynamics of that system in all of its complexity.
It is not only *what* the world is, but at any given time, *how* the
universe is—it is the essence and the totality of the world, yet it
is dependent on the context and the point of reference.†

In the Daoist tradition, there is no sense of causal determin-
ism in the universe; there is no sense of origin and no determined ending. The world is self-causing and self-effecting and
the individual is an intrinsic natural part of it, not an external
or objective part. In this non-teleological system individuals can
only go along with the order of the world and not attempt to
exert control over it.‡ The *Dao* is inherently non dialectical—it
is equally affected by action *(wei)* as much as inaction *(wu wei)*
and indeed, a core theme in the *Dao* is that inaction and the
negative is superior to action and the positive. The *Dao*, and
hence the world, is an interdependent, synergistic continuum
where each part is related to and has an effect on the other;
where the individual exists only in the context of the whole and
in its relationships to the greater continuum.

Whilst the various Chinese schools of thought have very different philosophical notions and practical manifestations, they
share the core objective of cultivating and attaining socio-political and natural *harmony*. The notion of harmony is a reflection
of the conditions of the age that gave rise to these philosophies
and it remains the central paradigm underlaying the psyche of
the Chinese world. From a synergy of these philosophies comes

* William H. Mott IV and Jae Chang Kim, *The Philosophy of Chinese Military Cul-
ture. Shih vs Li.* (Palgrave Macmillian, NY 2006). p8.
† Ames (1993), p50.
‡ *Ibid* p48.

the fundamental premise of Chinese thought — that the nature of all things, be they warfare, political, social, or natural order, is dynamic, holistic, constitutive and relative. The universe is bound in an interdependent web of interspatial, interpersonal and interphenomenal relationships in which harmony must be cultivated to understand the natural order of things and to attain order within it.* It is the cultivation of harmony and the search for order that is the fundamental premise that underlies Chinese strategic thought.

Harmony must be pursued and attained, and this is particularly true in politics, statecraft, and warfare. In the attainment of harmony, one must first understand the dynamic natural order of the interrelated universe. This understanding can only be achieved, if the process of attaining the understanding itself is known. The universe and the natural order is dynamic and ever changing and so by definition, it can not be known or understood as objective, definitive, or proscribed knowledge. Knowledge or understanding can only be derived out of this dynamic complexity by seeing and understanding the linkages and relatedness within that system through "intuition," "realisation," and "distillation." When the nature of order and the search for understanding and knowledge of that order has been intuited or realised, harmony (socio-political and strategic) can be attained. When the natural order of the universe is understood, both within oneself and within the enemy, then the "strategic advantage" can be sought and likewise understood in all of its dynamism and complexity.†

The convergence of these philosophical underpinnings in Chinese thought infuses strategic thought with a distinctive flavor in the way that this convergence is realised as a mechanism of action. The mechanism that is revealed in the classic texts is described as "*Shi* strategy." *Shi* strategy is the harmonious attainment of "strategic advantage" in the pursuit of national interests,

---

* After Ames (1993) p42.

† Roger T. Ames, *The Art of Rulership. A Study in Ancient Chinese Political Thought.* (University of Hawaii Press, Honolulu 1983). p66.

and it is shaped by a dynamic of four important forces.* The first of these forces is the *Dao*. The second is *shi* or "strategic advantage"—itself an abstract notion constituted from a combination of dynamic factors including conditions, circumstances, force, momentum, disposition, *etc*) which may be either tangible (*eg* physical, material, logistical) or intangible (*eg* temporal, spiritual, psychological). The third is *xing*, the tangible outward appearance of physical strength, such as strategic positions or power. The fourth is *li,* self interest or material gain that has a realist sense of priority, such as material, physical assets and outcomes, or in the modern parlance, "national interests."†

Accordingly, the pursuit of national interests is focused on the political ends rather than military results. At the level of grand strategy, military results, be they victory or defeat, are considered the means to an end, not the ends themselves.‡ The holistic nature of natural order considers the ruler or minister and the general as practitioners of the same profession of statecraft, pursuing a single unified political objective, though in different contexts. The "way" of Chinese strategic culture as received in the classic texts does not hold the Clausewitzian dichotomy of diplomacy as the exercise of politics and the exercise of strategy as war. Neither does it delineate strategy at grand (global geopolitics), national (military-economic power) or military (theater-tactical) levels. In the ideal of the classical Chinese tradition, the practitioners of statecraft act through a unifying reciprocity. Rulers and ministers should think as generals; generals should think as ministers, each intuiting their responses from the prevailing conditions in order to achieve the strategic advantage with a unifying effect.

---

* See Mott & Kim (2006) pp10-11 for a definition of *Shi*-strategy.

† See Ames (1993), pp72-84 and Mott & Kim (2006), for an extensive textual analyses of *Shi*-strategy in the classic strategic texts.

‡ Mott & Kim (2006) p13. The prime and most familiar example of this is the Vietnam War. Although the US demonstrated overwhelming technological superiority and tactical dominance, the North Vietnamese government and the National Liberation Front were willing to endure significant losses and tactical defeats - the means to the end – in order to realise an eventual strategic success in the political victory – the end itself.

Since the 1970s, much has been written on the nature of Chinese strategic culture as revealed by the classic texts, particularly in terms of the use of force, and the role of violence or war in grand strategy. While it is beyond the scope of this book to review this scholarship in depth, the consensus of much of this literature highlights three central concepts.* Most prominent of these has been described as the "pacifist bias of the Chinese tradition" that considered war as a "last resort," used only when all attempts of resolution has failed.† Complementing this "pacifist bias", is the "de-emphasis" of violence, with different scholarship citing instead, "anti-militarist bias" and a culture of "minimal violence," with an emphasis on non-violent stratagems such as psychological warfare and deception.‡ In this interpretation of Chinese strategic culture, when virtuous Confucian rule and governance had failed and the use of violent force had become unavoidable, the emphasis lay in "defensive and limited use of force".§

Any reading of the classic Chinese strategic texts does clearly and immediately reveal a general validity of this paradigm. There is a real ambivalence to the use of force in the classic Chinese texts, with a clear preference of other more elegant and less costly methods of non-violent force and coercion. In the *Sun Tzu,* the word *li* or force only appears nine times in total through out its thirteen chapters, often in a negative or cautionary context. In contrast, in *On War,* Clausewitz uses the word *gewalt* or force, eight times in two paragraphs alone where war is defined.¶ While this represents a generalized and idealized interpretation of the distinctiveness of Chinese strategic cul-

---

* For a comprehensive review of literature pertaining to the nature of the use of force in the Chinese strategic tradition, see Alistair Iain Johnston, *Cultural Realism. Strategic Culture and Grand Strategy in Chinese History.* (Princetone University Press, Princeton. 1995). pp62-69.

† John K. Fairbank, "Introduction: Varieties of the Chinese Military Experience", *Chinese Ways in Warfare,* Frank A. Kierman, Jr and John K. Fairbank, eds. (Harvard University Press, Cambridge. 1974). p.7.

‡ Johnston (1995). pp62-63.

§ *Ibid.* p64.

¶ Arthur Waldron, "The Art of Shi", *The New Republic,* June 23 1997, 216.25, p38.

ture, more recent scholarship suggests something other than a notion of a strategic culture of pacifism and of the reluctant use of violence by sagely ruler-philosophers.* A deeper reading and understanding of the classic texts, particularly in conjunction with readings in China's long military history reveals a much less romanticised picture. It is true that the classical strategists and their texts do emphasise concepts such as simple good government, virtuous rulership and non-violent methods such as deception, the building or disrupting of diplomacy, and alliance structures. However the essential fact remains that the Chinese strategists and philosophers of the Spring and Autumn Period and Warring States, were primarily concerned with war and statecraft in one of the bloodiest and most brutal periods of human history. The Spring and Autumn Period strategists and those that followed after them understood that war is an essential aspect of statecraft and politics—that war, like diplomacy, like alliances, and like espionage and deception, are simply the means to an end. This is however, not simply ascribing Chinese strategic thought on the side of universalist realism or at the very least, "cultural realism" and realpolitik; nor does it suggest that its practitioners are "West Point graduates who happen to speak another language".†

Contrary to the romanticized view, the use of force and violence is not simply used as a last resort when all other non-violent means have failed. Rather, it is a part of a wider set of strategic deliberations and its use is calculated for effect as merely one of many coordinated actions. It is not simply a moral or philosophical aversion to the use of force; it is also a practical one. War is costly in blood and treasure and this very fact is the basis of the entire process of strategic deliberation. This caveat is so important that it forms the first words of the *Sun Tzu*: "War is a vital matter of state. It is the field on

---

* *Ibid* p39.

† "Cultural realism" is the basis of Johnston's "*parabellum* paradigm". See Arthur Waldron's review of Johnston's *Cultural Realism. Strategic Culture and Grand Strategy in Chinese History. Ibid*, p38.

which life or death is determined and the road that leads to either survival or ruin, and must be examined with the greatest care."* All of the principles of Chinese strategic thought that have been interpreted as "anti-militarist" or "pacifist," such the minimisation of force, the preference of non-violent methods (diplomacy and disrupting alliances) are in fact, the preferred approach to managing conflict, with the express consideration of the preservation of one's own political legitimacy and support of the population, through the careful use of blood and treasure. In the Chinese way of war, it is much more efficient and much less costly to strike the enemy not at his physical or military center of gravity, but rather the center of gravity that counts the most—his sense of harmony and stability. The use of force is not avoided, but rather, it is minimized. It is simply one part of a greater holistic and adaptable strategy that includes all means of strategic maneuver.

When force is used, it is used to good effect by being quick, overwhelming, and decisive. It should leave the enemy in chaos and open to exploitation. Confused and in a state of physical, emotional, and strategic shock, the enemy would be in no condition to be able to react effectively to other strategic maneuvers, conducted in concert with the use of force.† Sun Tzu advises careful and considered use of force and cautions against anything less than a calculated and rational use of force: "A person in a fit of rage can be restored to good humour and a person in the heat of passion can be restored to good cheer, but a state that has perished cannot be revived, and the dead can not be brought back to life. Thus the farsighted ruler approaches battle with prudence and the good commander moves with caution. This is the way to keep the state secure and to preserve the army intact."‡ It is this inherent wisdom and the thread of *humanity* that runs throughout the classic Chinese texts, which resonates down through the centuries. It is central

---

* *Sun Tzu* Chapter 1 in Ames (1993), p103.
† Waldron (1997), p39.
‡ Sun Tzu Chapter 13 in Ames (1993) p166.

to the understanding that war is not an abstract concept, nor is it an exercise in engineering or an exercise in strategy like pins on a map, or pieces on a board. War is above all else, a social problem, a problem of humanity; a problem that requires social solutions and an understanding of humanity.

Sun Wu and *The Art of War of Sun Tzu*

The Art of War of Sun Tzu is the oldest and most well known and most studied of all strategic works. Known in Chinese as *Sun Zi Bingfa* or just simply as the *Sun Zi*, it is considered in East Asia and increasingly in the West as the foundation of strategic and military thought. The *Sun Tzu* is generally attributed to Sun Wu, a soldier-philosopher of the late of the Spring and Autumn Period and contemporary of Confucius. Sun Wu, better known by the honorific as Sun Tzu (Master Sun) is recorded by the Grand Historian of the Han Dynasty, Sima Qian in his monumental work of the *Shiji* (*The Records of the Grand Historian*), as being in the service of King Helu (544–496 BCE) of the state of Wu, some time around 512 BCE, where "in the west he defeated Chu and entered Ying. In the north, he overawed Qi and Jin and his name was known amongst the feudal lords, such was Sun Tzu's power amongst them."* Sun Wu was a member of a prominent clan famous for its expertise in the military arts, which includes his descendant Sun Bin who served King Wei of Qi during the Warring States. Sun Bin may have contributed to the editing of the *Sun Tzu* and subsequently added his own treatise to the canon, the *Sun Bin Bingfa (Sun Bin's The Art of War)* which was lost during the Han Dynasty, but subsequently rediscovered buried in Han Dynasty tombs (ca 140 BCE) in 1972 at Yin Que Shan.†

---

* See author's notes to Sadler's Introduction for Sun Tzu's famous "job interview" with King Helu of Wu. From Sima Qian, "*Sun Zi Wu Qi liezhuan*", *Shiji*. ("Sun Zi and Wu Qi. Biographies" *The Records of the Grand Historian*) vol 65. (109 BC to 91 BC). Zhonghua Publishing House, Beijing 1959.

† See Ames (1993) for detailed information of the Yin Que Shan archaeological texts.

Of the history of the text of *The Sun Tzu* itself, less is known although scholarly debate has raged from the Southern Song Dynasty (1127–1279 CE) until as late as the 20th century.* Some scholars take the traditional view and attribute the text to Sun Wu himself, whilst others ascribe multiple authorship and yet others consider the book a late fabrication.† The culmination of this long scholarship, in conjunction with the most recent archaeological and textual studies suggests that the *Art of War of Sun Tzu* can not be attributed directly to the hand of the historical Sun Wu. The fact that Sun Wu is referred to as "Master Sun" ascribes a hight degree of esteem and authority to the historical Sun Wu and suggests that the text was at least recorded by students of his arts.‡ Additionally, textual studies of the nature of military technology and the nature of warfighting, suggest that the text dates well into the Warring States Period sometime between 400–320 BCE.§ It is most likely that the core ideas of Sun Wu were transmitted by his students in the canonical tradition, with his thoughts recorded, copied down, commented upon, collated, and edited over several generations, in the same tradition as Confucius' *The Analects*, and the *Daodejing* of Lao Zi.¶ Archaeological evidence suggest however that the canonical form of the text had been essentially fixed into the present or received form by the early Han Dynasty, sometime around 140 -118 BCE.** The oldest extant scholarship of the present day received text dates to the commentaries of Cao Cao (155-220 CE), ruler, general, and scholar of the Later Han Dynasty.††

---

* See Ames (1993) pp20–31 and Sawyer (1993) p150 for a comprehensive review of the Sun Tzu authorship debate.

† Sawyer (1993) p150,

‡ Ames (1993) p24.

§ *Ibid*

¶ *Ibid* pp25-26

** *Ibid* p15

†† Cao Cao is immortalised in the Ming Dynasty novel *The Romance of the Three Kingdoms (Sanguo Yanyi)* by Luo Guanzhong.

The *Sun Tzu* is unquestionably the most "profound, comprehensive, and transcendent" of all strategic works.* It is the grand unifying text of conflict and statecraft, as its comprehensiveness draws and binds together every consideration for the successful and skilful conduct of conflict. The central premise of *Sun Tzu* is the key that war and all conflict functions and reacts as totality. The dynamism and interrelatedness of all things in the Chinese world view; phenomena, relations, space, and time, has driven a holistic approach to conflict, which is bound together in a common arc of strategic deliberation and maneuver, with little distinction or differentiation between warfighting and the fields of conflict that exist beyond the battlefield. The fields of government, diplomacy, alliances, psychological warfare, espionage, and economics, are all equal elements of a wider exercise of conflict and statecraft, which require coordination and control in order to achieve the maximum advantage or effect. This in turn drives a flexibility and adaptiveness in approach that is such a hallmark of *Sun Tzu*, and a freedom from the constraints of orthodoxy and dogma in practise. There are no taboos that must be observed, no institutional culture or mythological tradition to maintain—advance or retreat, regular or irregular troops, striking where least expected, creating deception and confusion, demonstrating strength and feigning weakness, talking peace in order to better position for victory—all are legitimate courses of action.

The *Sun Tzu* should not be seen as a field manual or instruction book but rather, as a "guide book," which may be used to point the reader in the right direction, but allow the reader to "read" the strategic situation and enact the most appropriate actions in order to gain the strategic advantage. This strategic tradition contained within *Sun Tzu* is above all else a knowledge culture, expressed as knowledge of the military arts, of the nature of government and of social order. Knowledge and awareness, the ability to understand the nature of

---

* Johnston (1995) p40.

things through discerning the rhythms and interactions of natural order is perhaps the most important skill in the *Sun Tzu*. Understanding the correlations and the linkages of the tangible and the intangible, the spiritual and the material is the key unifying factor and the enabler of an evaluative and controlled approach to war and conflict. Above all considerations, the *Sun Tzu* is about control. It is not control in the sense of a scientific teleological control, but rather, it is control in the Daoist tradition from which the *Sun Tzu* is firmly rooted.* It is the control of one's own actions through the understanding and mastery of situational awareness in the form of Daoist concepts such as *wei/wu wei* (using the dynamic of natural order through deliberate action or non-action) and "formlessness" which allows the most advantageous reaction to a given strategic problem.

Sima Rangju and
The Precepts of War by Sima Rangju

Sima Rangju was born of the clan Tian and named Tian Rangju. He served as Military Commander to Duke Jing (547-490 BCE) in the state of Qi.† Like Sun Wu, Sima Rangju was a contemporary of Confucius (551-479 BCE), who counselled Duke Jing of Qi when asked on the nature of government with: "Let the ruler act as a ruler, the minister as a minister, the father as a father, and the son as a son."‡

Sima Qian's biography of Sima Rangju in the *Shiji* relates the story of his appointment to the command of the army of Qi, after severe losses against the combined forces of Qin and

---

* See Coker (2003) *Ibid* and; Christopher Coker, *Waging War Without Warriors. The Changing Culture of Military Conflict.* (Lynne Rienner, Boulder. 2002), pp128-130. For detail of the inherent Daoism in Sun Tzu, see also Ames (1993) pp39-97 and Thomas Cleary, *The Art of War. Complete Texts and Commentaries. Sun Tzu, translated by Thomas Cleary.* (Shambala, Boston, 2000). pp4-29.

† Sima Qian, *"Sima Rangju liezhuan," Shiji.* ("Sima Rangju. Biography" *The Records of the Grand Historian),* vol 64 (109 to 91 BCE). Zhonghua Publishing House, Beijing 1959.

‡ Confucius, *The Analects* XII.11, Lau (1979).

Yan.* Sima Qian noted that Tian Rangju was a descendant of the son of Tian Wan's concubine. Tian Wan himself had been a commoner of the Chen clan and enfeoffed in the service of Duke Huan.† Thus not only was Tian Rangju descended from a commoner, he was also of relatively low status as the son of a concubine, as opposed to the son of the principal wife. Nevertheless, by virtue of his skill at arms and of his skill in civil affairs he was appointed as commanding general of the Qi armies. Distinguishing himself in battle as a strategist, a master of civil-military administration and as a humane and caring commander, Tian Rangju was appointed to the post of *Da Sima*, (Grand Master of Horse)—the Minister of War.‡ There after, his family was permitted to use the title as its name, and it is by this appellation that Sima Rangju is remembered.

This story from the *Shiji* reveals the depth of the social change that was sweeping China during the Spring and Autumn Period. As the political strife escalated into open warfare between the states, common men of ability such as Tian Wan and his descendant Sima Rangju began rising to power through merit and intrigue, as the established aristocracy lost the requisite vigour necessary for military, political, and personal survival. Accompanying the social mobility of that period was the growing professionalism in the conduct of affairs of state, in both the civil and military spheres, and the divergence between the two professions which had once solely been the domain of the aristocracy. The Tian clan could also claim the fame of the Sun family to its name. Tian Shu, also a descendant of Tian Wan was granted the family name of Sun in recognition of his achievements, so that Sun Wu and Sun Bin were members of the Tian clan.§ Ultimately in 384 BCE, the Tian clan gained enough power and capability that Duke Tai usurped the house of Jiang

---

* Sima Qian, "*Sima Rangju liezhuan,*" *Op. Cit.*

† Sawyer (1993) p441.

‡ This is the equivalent of the evolution of the word and military rank "Marshall" in European. By the Han Dynasty, Sima had become a common name, and remains one of the relatively few Chinese compound word (two character) family names.

§ Sawyer (1993) p411.

for the rule of the state of Qi. Qi was the last state to fall to the unification of the Qin in 221BCE.

Of the text of the *Sima Fa (The Methods of the Minister of War)*, Sima Qian questions ascribing the authorship to Sima Rangju, stating that: "There are many copies of the *Sima Bingfa* out in the world."* Like the biography of Sima Rangju himself, the *Sima Fa* reveals the nature of social and political change during the Spring and Autumn Period. The received text consists of a mere 5 chapters of the 155 reported during the Han Dynasty, though the received text has been transmitted in this form since the Tang Dynasty. Textual and historical scholarship suggests that the *Sima Fa* was probably complied from numerous sources from the time of the Eastern and Western Zhou era and latter amended by other contributors.†

The *Sima Fa* may be considered as a "handbook of government," in that it contains commentaries on the nature of war as policy, the practise of statecraft, domestic governance, civil-military relations and command principles. *Sima Fa* has a strong Confucian flavor and has been identified as a Confucian work, through its extensive commentary on attaining security through virtuous and moral government.‡ The core concepts and practises in the *Sima Fa* reflect those of the Eastern Zhou period, from which Confucius also based his thoughts and values. In the *Sima Fa*, these include the by then increasingly anachronistic values of moral and virtuous government and the importance of *li* or ritual propriety in the conduct of war. The discussions of civil administration and the role of the people, retain the civilizing themes of ethical and moral behaviour, even in time of war. In this sense, it is a part of the anachronistic world of Zhou civilization that was being lost.

Conversely, other concepts discussed in the text are indicative of the tidal forces of change sweeping the Spring and Autumn Period. Of these, most striking is the expression and

---

* Sima Qian, "*Sima Rangju liezhuan*", *Op.cit.*
† Sawyer (1993) p115.
‡ Johnston (1995) p42.

justification of the use of force or "righteous war" as an instrument of policy, in addition to commentary stemming from the growing professionalization, specialization, and divergence of civil administration and the military arts.* Of particular significance is the very modern emphasis on training and preparation, military administration and management. Although the *Sima Fa* lacks the literary and intellectual beauty of the *Sun Tzu* and instead reads in a very practical manner, it nevertheless contains the thread of the consciousness and primacy of humanity that unites the different schools of Chinese strategic thought and the military arts.

Reconciling these opposing themes, there is a subtext of historical narrative of the decline of civilization and the rise of war, which runs throughout the *Sima Fa*. This begins with descriptions of the perfect, virtuous, and harmonious rule of the mythical rulers of antiquity who pacified and organized the world by their benevolence and virtue. They were exemplars of ethical and moral behaviour that was to be celebrated and advocated by the later Confucians. From these perfect sovereigns, the *Sima Fa* then continues to describe the righteous use of force by the subsequent sage kings during the Xia and Shang Dynasties who needed to bring order and justice to their realms, in response to unvirtuous and unethical vassals. Finally the *Sima Fa* discusses the decline of virtue in the latter part of the Zhou Dynasty, and the absolute necessity of the military arts under these (contemporary) conditions.

Wu Qi and *Wu Zi on the Art of War*

Wu Qi was born around 430BCE in the state of Wei and according to Sima Qian, was a student of Zeng Zi, one of Confucius' founding students.† Accordingly his treatise on war has been

---

* See Alistair Iain Johnston's discussion on "righteous war" and the use of force *Ibid* pp126-130.

† Sima Qian, "*Sun Zi Wu Qi liezhuan*" *Op.cit.* Sawyer (1993) pp198-201 details a wide range of biographical scholarship of Wu Qi beyond Sima Qian, and suggest that

described as revealing Confucian realist and Legalist elements.* This is very much in keeping with the intellectual development of the Confucian school of thought throughout the Spring and Autumn Period and the Warring States, when the text of the *Wu Zi* (*Wu Zi on The Art of War*) was compiled by Wu Qi and later added to and edited by his students.† Sima Qian's extensive biography of Wu Qi, later known along with his treatise as Wu Zi (Master Wu), reveals much of the philosophical basis of Wu Qi's work. In the *Shiji,* Sima Qian recounts that Wu Qi killed his wife, a native of the state of Qi in order to prove his reliability to the state of Lu, which wanted to appoint him as commander against the armies of Qi. A detractor who hated Wu Qi then stated: "Wu Qi is a cruel and suspicious man." The detractor recalled that when Wu Qi was young, he ruined his family by spending its fortune in a vain bid to seek an official appointment. When his neighbors laughed at him, he killed more than thirty of them and fled. On leaving, he bit his mother's arm swearing: "Until I am appointed as a minister, I will not return to Wei." He then went to study with Zeng Zi, but he had only been there a short time when his mother died, but he did not return home to mourn. Zeng Zi despised him for this lack of filial piety and severed his relationship with him. After this he went to the state of Lu to study the art of war.

While modern scholarship casts a dubious light on the unflattering character of Wu Qi sketched in the *Shiji,* Sima Qian's characterisation of Wu Qi does in fact complement the nature of his work contained within the *Wu Zi* text.‡ Wu Qi's biography depicts him as being rooted in the fundamentals of Confucian tradition, but pragmatic enough not to be beheld to "dogmatic" Confucianism when circumstances required. On

---

chronologically, it is more likely that Wu Qi was a student of Zeng Zi's son.

  * Johnston (1995) p41.

  † Confucius was the originator of the Confucian tradition, which diversified through the works of Confucian students such as Mencius, from whose thoughts the received orthodox tradition belongs; and Xun Zi, whose (later deemed) heterodox Confucianism gave rise to the Legalist school of thought.

  ‡ See Sawyer (1995) p196.

the one hand, Wu Qi breaks the most sacred of Confucian duties by failing to perform the funeral and mourning rites for his mother, yet in doing so, he demonstrates his faithfulness in keeping his vow to her. Similarly, Wu Qi kills his own wife in order to demonstrate his reliability to the state, yet he advocates in his thoughts the Confucian idea of benevolence of government and administration.* Further still, Sima Qian further characterises Wu Qi's Confucian virtue and his unwavering sense of morality as a commander by his behaviour in the field. Wu Qi wore the same clothes as his men, ate the same food as they did, slept on the ground, and on the march did not ride a horse or chariot. He enduring the privations and simplicities of his troops in the field, and eschewed the luxuries and comforts befitting his rank and station as the commanding general. The result of this inspired leadership by example notes Sima Qian, was the unquestioning loyalty and faith in Wu Qi from the ranks who followed him to their deaths.†

---

* Sawyer (1995) p191.

† Sima Qian, *Shiji*, *"Sun Zi Wu Qi liezhuan" Op.cit.* These leadership qualities are reminiscent of the leadership of the Red Army, during China's civil war of 1927-1937 and 1945-1949. The leadership of the Red Army (eventually falling to Mao Zedong and Zhu De) held few distinctions in rank or station. Officers shared the privations of the war, particularly in the first part of the civil war, when the Red Army was out numbered and out gunned. During the year long fighting retreat of the Long March 1936-1937 particularly, the Red Army/Communist Party leadership suffered the same hardships as the ranks. The Long March traversed some 12,500 km over a 12 month period, covering high mountains, marsh lands, and deserts of south western, western, and north western regions of China. Of the 80,000 men who broke out of encirclement in 1936, only 8,000 survivors arrived at Yanan in 1937, the rest having fallen casualties to enemy action, succumbing to nature, or having deserted. This common bond of the survivors was to be the glue that held the Chinese Communist Party together for decades afterwards. In the re-building phase at Yanan 1937-1945, Mao Zedong's egalitarian socio-military policies, skilled use of propaganda, and political education in addition to the leadership by example, further emphasized this bond between officers and men, which drew thousands and then hundreds of thousands of peasants and intellectuals to the Communist Party's cause. The Red Army, later re-named the People's Liberation Army swelled to some 1 million at the resumption of war in 1945. Kuomintang Prisoners of War were treated humanely and offered the choice of joining the PLA or being paroled home. Rather than returning to the corrupt, uncaring, and inept KMT armies of Chiang Kai-shek, hundreds of thousands joined the PLA. By time of the retreat of the KMT to Taiwan, the PLA had grown to some 4 million men.

The *Wu Zi* is perhaps the most tangible of the three classic texts, in that it easily reconciles its inherent philosophical concepts with strategic considerations. It further reconciles the philosophy/strategy nexus with the practical challenges of the political legitimacy of government, the nature of government policy and of civil-military administration, management, and leadership at a time of war. Wu Qi's study of Confucianism under Zeng Zi reveals itself throughout the *Wu Zi*. In it, Wu Qi advocates the fundamentals of Confucian virtue: propriety and ritual, benevolence and righteousness as the cornerstone of government and civil administration.* This reflects Wu Qi's grasp of the reality of the times and the evolving nature of warfare, from the aristocratic "sport of kings" to that of total war.

As peasants became conscripted to the wars, Wu Qi realised that the war effort increasingly demanded the acquiescence and fundamental support for the state from the ordinary people. To Wu Qi, state security and stability was fundamentally based on a harmonious state, ruled through Confucian virtues such as benevolence, and motivated to war only after virtuous and righteous deliberation. A state that had the moral support of the people through its wise rule would be capable of enduring the shock of war and supporting the state in its time of need. Wu Qi successfully reconciled this "soft" Confucianism with a harder edged Confucian realism, by understanding that virtuous and benevolent rule through a well educated civil administration meant absolutely nothing in a dangerous security environment, without an efficiently trained, well led, and capable army. Therefore not only would the people offer their moral support to the state in a time of war, they would also actively and willing contribute to the total war effort, confident in victory of its virtuously led army. Accordingly, Wu Qi wrote extensively on the need for well organised, well trained, well motivated men, led by carefully selected officers assigned to duties in accordance with their demonstrated capabilities.

---

* Sawyer (1995) p198.

In this deep and broad understanding of the critical importance of the "human factor" in warfare, Wu Qi demonstrates a remarkably modern system of coordination in civil-military leadership and organization. The central thread of the "human factor" in the Chinese way of war, exemplified in the works of the *Wu Zi, Sun Tzu,* and *Sima Fa,* would echo down through the millennia, as they shaped the destinies of millions and redrew the political maps of East Asia time and time again. When we think about the politico-military brilliance and success of 20th Century soldiers-scholar such as Mao Zedong, and Võ Nguyên Giáp, we see the legacy of the *Wu Zi, Sun Tzu,* and *Sima Fa.* In the strategic considerations of the 21st Century, we see them still.

Chinese Strategic Thought in the West

The 1980s saw the nexus of two significant phenomena, as the Western world came to face the economic and strategic landscape of the final decades of the 20th century. Both phenomena, one military and the other economic, led the West to an initial and then to an avalanche in the need and desire to digest and understand the classical precepts of Chinese strategic thought.

The first was the scholarly and strategic self-evaluation after some 30 years of Western engagement in, or observation of East Asian conflicts. By the mid-1970s it became increasingly clear to some analysts that there were perhaps distinctive culturally based approaches to strategy in war and in diplomacy.

Most important was the evaluation in the aftermath of the debacle of the Vietnam War, where paradoxically, overwhelming American technological superiority and oft repeated tactical dominance was unable to affect the ultimate outcome of the North Vietnamese victory in 1975. Indeed, time and time again, the adaptability and fluidity of North Vietnamese strategic thought allowed them to take tactical or even strategic defeats in the field, such as the failure of general uprising in South Vietnam during the Tết Offensive of 1968, and turn them into strategic advantage on the equally crucial battlefields of international public opinion and diplomacy.

In fighting the Vietnam War, the United States tended to view the war as a problem to be solved with a military means and measured through statistical calculations. It fought the war with the application of firepower and technology in the conduct of a strategy of "attrition," measuring progress by statistical indicators such as the "body count."[*] Some time after the war, an American Colonel boasted to his Vietnamese counterpart: "You know, you never defeated us on the battlefield." To this the Vietnamese Colonel replied: "That may be so, but that is also irrelevant".[†] The military strategy was only one part of a wider war, and not the one the necessarily mattered the most.[‡] In contrast the Vietnamese fought the war as a totality, using either co-ordinated strategies or simply using serendipity to advantage. The totality of war combined military strategy with psychological strategy and political strategy.[§] After the war, the principle architect of the offensive, General Võ Nguyên Giáp stated: "For us, you know, there is no such thing as a single strategy. Ours is always a synthesis, simultaneous military, political, and diplomatic."[¶] It was a co-ordination of conventional war and insurgency, combined with psychological strategy, in the villages and towns of South Vietnam and on the TV screens and streets of the United States. It combined political strategy, in Vietnam and on the stage of international diplomacy. The ultimate victory, some two years after the withdrawal of US Forces, under the Paris Peace Accords of 1973 marked the ultimate strategic failure of the long term American mission of preserving the South Vietnamese government and for which it

---

[*] Stanley Karnow, *Vietnam. A History.* (Penguin Books, NY. 1991), p18.

[†] Karnow, (1991) p19.

[‡] The success on the battlefield during Tết 1968 was a poisoned chalice – its images of death, destruction and brutality on American TV was a major factor in turning American public support away from the war and ultimately precipitating an American withdrawal.

[§] Mark McNeilly, *Sun Tzu and the Modern Art of Warfare,* Oxford University Press, New York. 2001. p12.

[¶] Karnow (1991) p548.

had paid a cost of some hundreds of billion dollars and over 58,000 young American lives.

Of the Chinese behaviour in the Sino-Vietnamese War of 1979, Western observers were perplexed. After a large scale cross border invasion into Vietnam, and after suffering tens of thousands of casualties in the three week campaign, Chinese forces withdrew unilaterally across the border after seizing decisive terrain at Long Son and securing the path to Hanoi and without securing any political concessions from Vietnam.* While Western observers noted that the Chinese were unable to achieve the ostensible goal of forcing the withdrawal of Vietnamese troops from Cambodia, China's client state, the Chinese claimed that they had achieved their goal of "teaching Vietnam a lesson." Western observers were puzzled by the incongruity of the tactical successes gained against the lack of any obvious strategic advantage in the withdrawal, beyond demonstrating that China was able to "disrupt Soviet strategic calculations" and "put restraint on the wild ambitions of the Vietnamese and to give them a limited lesson".†

For Western analysts, this behaviour paralleled Chinese actions during the Sino-Indian War of 1962. After launching an offensive in the Aksai Chin and Arunachal Pradesh regions of the border, the Chinese declared a unilateral ceasefire and withdrawal after having reached the maximum extent of the Chinese claim lines of the territorial dispute on the Indian side of the pre-war "Line of Actual Control." Chinese forces withdrew back to their original pre-war positions on the Line of Actual Control, after defeating all Indian forces in the disputed territories on the Indian side of the border. At this point the Chinese unilaterally returned all Indian Prisoners of War, and returned their small arms and support weapons—cleaned and in good working order.‡ Similarly the motivation of this trade of a clear

---

* Mott and Kim (2006) p5.

† Zbigniew Brzezinski, *Power and Principle: Memoirs of the National Security Advisor, 1977-1981*, (Farra Straus Giroux, 1983) p409.

‡ Mott & Kim (2006) p5.

strategic and tactical advantage was perplexing, especially so as
the Chinese had exchanged the advantage for a return to the *status quo* position and its resolution by diplomatic means. Despite
a number of skirmishes in the mid to late 1960s, the dispute was
eventually settled via diplomatic means as late as 1996.

Going back earlier, Western powers were surprised time and
time again at the strategy, tactics, and successes of East Asian
forces at war with each other and with the West. The victory
of the Việt Minh over the French in the First Indochina War
was a surprise. The unexpected entry of China's forces into the
Korean War, and the inability of American technological superiority to force the less well armed and technologically inferior
enemy beyond the stalemate was a surprise. The defeat of Chiang Kai-shek's well armed and technologically superior forces
by Mao Zedong's People's Liberation Army, with its peasant
guerrilla origins was a surprise. Earlier still, the tactical brilliance of Admiral Isoruku Yamamoto's strike on Pearl Harbor
was a surprise, as was the Japanese warrior ethic of no surrender, the "banzai charge," and the *kamikaze* attack.

In this climate of reflection in the 1980s, in the evaluation of
the strategic failure of Vietnam, scholars and strategists particularly in the United States were rapidly coming to terms with the
challenge to the notion of the infallibility of the orthodoxy of
the Western "way of war." This was a challenge to the "Western way," particularly on a number of fronts: firstly it was a
challenge to the rationalist notion of supremacy and efficacy
of technology as a deciding factor; secondly, it was a challenge
to the Jominian notion of force as the instrument of decisive
victory; thirdly, it was a challenge to the ethnocentric paradigm
of rationalist Western strategic thought.

In this crucible, the study of "strategic culture" was born,
as scholars and strategist sought to understand the notion of
the influence of culture on national approaches to conflict and
strategy.* Strategic culture can be defined as "the body of beliefs

---

* For a review of the intellectual development of the birth of the study of strategic

that guides and circumscribes thought on strategic questions, influences the way strategic issues are formulated, and sets the vocabulary and the perceptual parameters of strategic debate."[*]
In the aftermath of the Vietnam War, General Maxwell Taylor, former US Chairman of the Joint Chiefs of Staff, paraphrased Sun Tzu as he reflected on the involvement in the war: "First, we didn't know ourselves. We thought that we were going into another Korean war, but this was a different country. Secondly, we didn't know our South Vietnamese allies. We never understood them, and that was a surprise. And we knew less about North Vietnam. Who was Ho Chi Minh? Nobody really knew. So, until we know the enemy and know our allies and know ourselves, we'd better keep out of this kind of dirty business. It's very dangerous."[†]

The second phenomena driving the need to understand Chinese strategic thought was the East Asian economic miracle; the meteoric rise of the economic power houses of Japan, South Korea, and Taiwan, with China herself then slowly stirring to life under a remarkable plan of transformation and modernization. In East Asia, business leaders have long translated Sun Tzu's thoughts from the realm of statecraft to the battlefield of business. In the face of the East Asian economic miracle, Western business leaders sought for an understanding of the basis of East Asian economic and business thought.

At the cusp of "the Asian Century," Sun Tzu's famous maxim of the need to "know the enemy" has seen Chinese strategic thought enter the mainstream of Western business and military consciousness. So much so, that Sun Tzu can be found not only dispensed as "fortune cookie wisdom" in quotations in military field manuals and doctrinal pamphlets, but also in books on economic and financial strategy. From the early 1980s, driven

---

culture in the West, see Johnston (1995) pp 1-32.
   [*] This definition was the given by Jack Synder who coined the term "strategic culture" in 1977. Jack Synder, *The Soviet Strategic Culture:Implications for Nuclear Options.* (Rand R-2154-AF, Santa Monica) in Johnstone (1995), p5.
   [†] Karnow (1991) p23.

in part by business strategy, in part by the post-Vietnam evaluation, Chinese strategic thought, in the guise of the *Sun Tzu*,
became an industry in its own right, with a bewildering number
of translations, commentaries, and interpretations published
(perhaps some 30-plus versions). Amid the plethora of "Sun
Tzu for the business world" books and Asian business consul-
tants dispensing their own Sun Tzu based "fortune cookie wisdom," Sun Tzu even made an appearance in Hollywood, where
Oliver Stone's *Wall Street* featured pithy punch lines from *Sun
Tzu* by its Wall Street players.

Pre-modern Classics for Post-modern War

The absolute necessity of a deeper cultural understanding
of the enemy and of the environment in which armies must
fight perhaps reached a point of maturation in the West in and
around 2007, after some thirty years of critical post-Vietnam
evaluation and driven directly by the necessity of providing
an *effective* response to the counterinsurgency in Iraq. In his
deployment to command the Multi-National Force in Iraq,
General David Petraeus PhD, put together an expert group of
sociologist, anthropologist, and other social scientist "soldier-
scholars," most notably Lieutenant Colonel David Kilcullen
PhD of the Australian Army. Petraeus and his team identified
the most effective response to the counterinsurgency as being
rooted on the fundamental premise that an effective response
to a conflict environment can only be one which is based on
a deeper cultural understanding of the nature of the conflict
and the social problems that lie at its heart. The resulting "cultural turn" within the American military in the war effort in
both Iraq and Afghanistan, has led to a heightened sense of
the need for a true understanding of cultural knowledge and
"conflict ethnography" in the approaches to counterinsurgency
warfare.* Indeed the US Army 2006 *Counterinsurgency: Field*

---

* David Kilcullen, "Religion and Insurgency" May 12, 2007. *Small Wars Journal*

Manual FM 3-24 written with significant contribution from "the Petraeus guys," stresses the critical importance of cultural knowledge and the central role of culture in the nature of society and conflict.[*]

It is the nature of 21st century "postmodern war" itself, combining elements of both modern and pre-modern war which requires a critical and complete understanding of war and strategy contained in the classic Chinese strategic texts.[†]

The nature of warfare in the 21st century marks a nexus of a number of critical sociological, political, and strategic trends, driven by the key factor of the Information Technology revolution. With the end of the "modern" or industrial age, the "postmodern" or information age, with its multiplicity of layers of connectivity, has in conjunction with the forces of globalization and the post Cold War international security environment, irrevocably changed the nature of warfare as well as the conflict environment.

One of the greatest effects of the IT revolution has been globalization and the rise of the "Third Age" where the creation and exploitation of knowledge is the dominant force in civilization, giving rise to new forms of economies, wealth creation, media dissemination, forms of families, and politics.[‡] Globalization has resulted in a real-time connectivity of economies and information across the spectrum of boundaries, be they trans-national, physical, institutional boundaries or cultural boundaries. The effect of globalization is that it has intensified transnational economic interdependency so that effectively, states need each other more than they ever have, making the wars between states less likely than ever before. However, one

---

Blog. http://smallwarsjournal.com/blog/2007/05/religion-and-insurgency/

[*] See particularly Chapter 3, US Army, *Counterinsurgency: Field Manual 3-24* (Government Printing Offices, Washington), 2006.

[†] Thomas Kane articulates the idea that in the age of "postmodern war," it is necessary to consider "pre-modern" (pre-scientific, pre-industrial) as well as modernist (technologically and industrial) approaches to warfare and strategy. Thomas M. Kane, *Ancient China on Postmodern War. Enduring Ideas From the Chinese Strategic Tradition.* (Routledge, Abingdon) 2007 p5.

[‡] See Alvin Toffler, *The Third Wave* (Bantam) 1980.

of the critical aspects of globalization is that it is not fully controllable by governments. In many ways, global forces such as public opinion, consumer advertizing, and demand can be driven by non-governmental actors such as multi-nationals and transnational corporations, media corporations, even private individuals or other non-state actors such as religious, revolutionary, and activist groups. Similarly, there is a lack of information control. Information is not only freely available, but it is there for anyone to gather, invent, disseminate, and interpret in one's own way and for one's own means. Globalization has changed the distribution of power, both political and economic, within and between states, markets, and civil society.*

At the same time, the international security environment in the post Cold War era has seen seismic changes, both in the balance of the modern age Westphalian state-centric international system; as well as a fragmentation of the world map along premodern lines. While the fall of the Soviet Union in 1991 resulted in a "unipolar moment" of the United States, the ascendance of a more assertive European Union, of the "Rising China," and a resurgent Russia has seen changing dynamics of security in the early 21st century. At the same time, the fall of the Soviet Bloc, in concert with the continued process of decolonization from the Imperial era, has seen a fracturing of many states and societies, reverting back to distinctly pre-modern religious and sectarian lines. In concert with the decline of the state itself, there has been an associated rise of sub-state and non-state actors, paradoxically, often with a high level of organization and structure as well as unity of information and message, provided by the connectivity and reach of the globalized IT system.

This international dichotomy has resulted in yet another paradox. The states themselves have reached new heights of military capability through the IT revolution, as weapons technology has achieved great heights not only in destructivity but

---

* Michael Evans, "Military Theory and Practise in the 21st Century," in *Future Armies, Future Challenges. Land warfare in the information age.* Michael Evans, Russell Parkin, and Alan Ryan eds. (Allen & Unwin, Sydney) 2004 p28

also in accuracy. However, in the globalised interdependency, states are ever less likely to go to war against each other, as the constraints imposed by the web of interconnectivity of economies and public opinion serve to create shared vital interests between states and societies.

The strategic environment of the 21ˢᵗ Century is predicated more on sociological problems rather than the application of the revolution in military technology and its use in combat. This new strategic environment is described as the "nontrinitarian" or "post–Clausewitz" age, to signify the end of the dominance of the state and the trinity of the state in warfare.* The 21ˢᵗ Century strategic environment is rather more a fragmentary complex of socio-political conflict, where the modern demarcations of the civil and military world have become blurred. This complexity of conflict brought on by the convergence of the civil and military realms in the IT revolution has been described as "Third Wave War," and as "new wars" (predominantly insurgencies and low-intensity conflicts) to distinguish them from the "old wars" of Clausewitzian warfare.† While these types of warfare have characterized the post-colonial period and the proxy wars of the Cold War, the concept of "new war" refers to war in the era of globalization, and its phenomena of interconnectivity and transnational connectiveness. It is this interconnectivity of the world and the globalized, decentralized privatization process that has led to the erosion of the autonomy of the state and of the monopoly of the state in the conduct of organized violence. This is witnessed by the proliferation of self or externally funded ethnic and religious militias, armed criminals and terrorists. These "new wars" are based on the reclamation of the political power of identities, be they tribal,

---

* Martin van Creveld. *On Future War*, (Brassy's London 1991) p53.

† See Alvin Toffler and Heidi Toffler. *War and Anti-War. Making Sense of Today's Global Chaos*. (Warner Books, London, 1993). Toffler and Toffler described "Third Wave War," to distinguish it from the First Wave (world of agrarian and feudal) wars and Second Wave industrial wars *Ibid;* and Mary Kaldor who describes "new wars": Mary Kaldor, *New and Old Wars. Organised Violence in a Global Era*. (Stanford University Press 1999) p3.

religious, or national.* This process of the growing irrelevance of the state and the rise of identity politics is indicative of a general trend in the socio-political aspect of conflict.

The beginning of the post Cold War world was characterized by the decline of the "artificial" states constructed during the period from the 1920s to the 1960s. The decline of the national constructs of post-Imperial Europe and the post-colonial and client states of Asian and Africa, were marked by the deconstruction of both social and political order. Ranging in magnitude from the decline of order in Indonesia to catastrophic collapse of the state in the USSR and most particularly Yugoslavia, these deconstructions were centred on the conflict of identity, both ethnic and religious. The end of ideological conflict of the Cold War and the collapse of the "artificially" created states gave way to more deep rooted and "visceral" motivations of conflict, many of which were masked by the ideological and post-colonial nationalist constructs of the previous age.

This illustrates yet another paradox in the international dichotomy. While international relations and grand strategy of the states are predicated on the Western notions of realpolitik, beyond the Western world, or at least those states that operate as part of the Westphalian system, the causes of war transcend calculated or rational considerations.† Pre-modern considerations such as faith, ethnicity, and identity, re-kindled by the rise of modern tribalism have already demonstrated that war will take a very different form from the familiar Western patterns of the last 300 years. In this post-Westphalian age, conflict resembles that of the pre-Westphalian age, where visceral tribal loyalties of faith and identity will supplant strategic realist agendas.‡

The blurring of civil-military lines has been a changing trend since the height of the Westphalian and Industrial ages in the period from the Franco-Prussian war to the Great War. This period marked the height of the civil-military distinction, with the

---

* *Ibid* p69.
† van Creveld (1991) p155.
‡ *Ibid* p198.

development of international conventions governing the civil-military distinction and the rules of war by combatants. By the time of World War II, this distinction had devolved in the face of total war and the needs of national survival and the survival of identity. State campaigns of the strategic bombing of civil populations and of genocide, both conducted at an industrial scale, destroyed the last vestiges of chivalric notions inherent in the conventions of war. This notion reached its heights in the nuclear age of mutual assured destruction. The proliferation of the use of force by non-state militias and the proliferation of weapons, both small arms and weapons systems, has shifted the emphasis of warfare from the Clausewitzian standard of force on force conflict, to that of "force on population" or "population on population."

In the conduct of "new wars" practices "discarded by the West for the last 300 years" such as attacking civil populations, attacking heads of state, attacking cultural monuments, and holding entire populations to ransom, have reappeared.[*] These visceral notions derived from the conduct of conflict at its most elementary form, that is, war against the "other" was the behavioural norm in the West in the pre-Westphalian age. This behavioural norm has indeed, never entirely disappeared. Rather it has merely been masked behind the fact that conflict in the Western consciousness has been culturally Euro-centric, as if the war crimes committed by Serbs against Bosnians were any less abhorrent than those of Hutus against Tutsis, or of Cambodians against each other. Conflict with the "cultural other" and the visceral savagery that accompanies it largely disappeared with the end of the religious conflicts of the Thirty Years War. In the period that followed, European conflict centered on Clausewitzian conflict which tempered the civil savagery of conflict as the civil-military distinction rose to pre-eminence amongst states which shared these cultural value systems.[†]

---

[*] van Creveld (1991) p203.
[†] *Ibid* p204.

Yet elsewhere, in non-Western European liberal democratic cultural systems, the civil-military delineation has never taken hold, as the Western horror of the conduct of other cultures in postmodern wars attests. We know, because we watched them. The ten years following the fall of the Soviet Union saw not the realization of a utopian "New World Order," but rather suicide bombers in the form of women and children, hijacked jetliners used as precision guided munitions, fantasies of a pan-national Caliphate, and even re-emergence of "ethnic cleansing" in the heart of Europe itself—all live on CNN. This is the reversionary nature of warfare and conflict in the 21st Century, where conflict is reverting back to a more "primitive state" of irrational, visceral motivations and more distressingly, in the conduct of conflict itself.

The re-emergence of tribal and identity politics, free of Clausewitzian realism has significant implications. If conflict is rooted in non-rational and visceral concerns of identity and belief, then by implication, the conduct and resolution of conflict must follow these lines and be resolved along these lines. If the 1991 Gulf War was the last "modern or 3rd Generation War," then the "War on Terror" marks the first "postmodern or 4th Generation War." The "War on Terror" at its core, visceral level is not being fought over geo-political power, but rather over culture. The World Trade Center attacks of September 11, 2001 were in the minds of the attackers attacks on the symbols of the worst materialist excesses of Western culture, embodied in the Twin Towers located in the heart of New York's financial district.[*]

Under these technological and sociological conditions, the *conflict environment* of 4th Generation War is marked by four critical factors: Complexity, Diversity, Diffusion, Lethality.[†]

---

[*] See John Carroll. "Twin Towers Revisited. A Culutral Interpretation of Modern Terrorism". *Australian Army Journal*. Vol I, No.2, (Land Warfare Studies Center, Australian Army, Canberra) p61.

[†] This concept of 4th Generation War is after the Australian Army's concept of "complex warfighting." For detail, see LTCOL Dave Kilcullen, *Complex Warfighting*, (Future Land Warfare Center, Australian Army. Canberra 2004).

The complexity of 4ᵗʰ Generation War creates an indistinct and ambiguous environment, where conflict is no longer the domain of uniformed, state based military forces. There are hostile forces such militias, insurgents, and armed criminal organizations who all contend for power alongside state sponsored militias, irregulars, and "private armies" as well as armed civilians. This conflict environment is further complicated with the addition "friendly" forces such as NGOs, government agencies such as elements of foreign ministries, police, security, and intelligence services, each pursuing different objectives, not necessarily in a unified or co-ordinated manner with each other or with the "friendly" armed forces. In addition there are neutral onlookers, vested interests groups and critics, often in the form of the media, the UN, business interests, and academics, who have significant influence on international and local public opinion, or who can be in turn, influenced by the combatants in the creation of public opinion. Finally, there is the complexity in the physical terrain of diverse physical environments, often in close association with the human and anthropological terrain. This results in a complex of ethno-linguistic and spatial distributions which has significant impact on the dynamics of conflict environments, and operational actions.

4ᵗʰ Generation War is also characterised by a diversity of threats. The civilianization of conflict means that in addition to armed combatants, computer hackers, smugglers, protestors, environmentalists, multinational and transnational business interests, state based diplomatic alliances, religious sects, *et al*, all have the potential to affect national security and provide challenges to state based responses. These actors both state and non-state, seek to use asymmetric methods to effect changes in political will and domestic opinion. Under these conditions, tactical victories can translate into strategic losses.

With the convergence of state and non-state actors, warfare has become diffuse, with a breakdown between strategic and operational levels and a blurring of civil-military relations and command. This serves also to break down the distinction between combatants and non-combatants, as the lines between the battlefield and the home front are removed, particularly in insurgencies and counterinsurgencies and loose concepts such as the "global war on terror." In an age of terrorism and counterterrorism, war has diffused into peacetime, as the battlefront has shifted to the home front itself, where government approaches in distant operations have distinct and immediate consequences at home. Finally, 4th Generation War is characterised by its lethality, as technology has made weapons more precise and more lethal, while the global proliferation of arms has placed the availability of weapons within the reach of any actor who has the ability to pay for them.

This complex conflict environment has resulted in a number of critical trends in 4th Generation War. These are:

The compression of war at the operational level. ie *tactical operations* have *strategic implications*, given the access of media with global coverage, direct from the front line, and the effect on international and domestic public opinion.

Conventional warfighting is not the deciding factor in war. Warfighting is now a series of complex problems in a complex terrain and a complex human environment.

Wars can be won or lost by strategic effects that do not involve warfighting. Strategic effects can include: The effective management of cultural and ethnological sensitivities; the careful management of international and domestic public opinion through media and information; the effective synchronization of diplomatic, NGO, and non-institutional actors and the strength of the moral high ground.

A holistic approach to constitutive factors are the key to managing conflict, where "managing" does not necessarily mean "winning."

Postmodern or 4th Generation War, is the age of the "strategic corporal," where command responsibility has devolved to relatively junior leaders in the age of instant communication and media. The strategic corporal must not only be an expert leader and decision maker in warfighting, but also across the spectrum of "military operations, other than war" such as humanitarian operations, peace operations, and even public relations. In the age of the strategic corporal, the decisions and actions of a junior leader based on his or her skills in warfighting, mediation, cultural awareness, the laws of armed conflict, civil and international law—all in the glare of the media—can have profound and strategic military-political consequences that can affect the outcome of a mission and on the reputation of his country.*

The complexity of 4th Generation War brought about by the paradoxical relationship of the interconnectivity and the divisiveness of the information age, results in complex solutions to the prevention, conduct, and resolution of conflict and warfare. In the post-industrial and post-Clausewitzian world, "anti-war" is a complex response of strategic applications of political, economic, military, and cultural power, which involves all sectors of society and with a "Whole of Government" approach.[†]

Understanding the nature of the cultural other is critical for the understanding of the way the other views the world, and the conduct and ultimate resolution of conflict. Devolved of Clausewitzian realism, understanding the view of conflict and the conduct of warfare of an adversary will depend on understading his innate cultural responses. The key to strategic success in the modern age, is not the study and mastery of technology. It is the study of the minds of humanity and mastery of the understanding of an adversary. Strategist Ralph Peters stated in 1998 that "We must study the minds and souls of violent men, seeking to understand them on a level that our civilization has avoided for 2,000 years....In this age of technological miracles, our military needs to study mankind."[‡]

---

* Major Lynda Liddy, "The Strategic Corporal. Some Requirements in Training and Education," *The Australian Army Journal* Vol II No2 (Australian Army Land Warfare Studies Center. Canberra) 2005 p140.

† See Toffler & Toffler's description of "anti-war" *Op.cit* p3.

‡ Ralph Peters, "Our New Old Enemies," in *Challenging the United States Symmetrically and Asymmetrically: Can America Be Defeated?* Lloyd J. Matthews, ed. (US Army War College Strategic Studies Institute, Carlisle PA July 1998) p215.

So here we come full circle back to the wisdom and the importance of our pre-modernist Chinese strategic texts, with Sun Tzu's maxim of "Know your enemy and know yourself, in one hundred battles you will never be defeated" echoing across two thousand years. In post-modern war, armed and equipped with modern technologies alongside pre-modern motivations and situation complexities, the inherent truth of Chinese strategic thought—that wars are not won exclusively on the battlefield, but equally and more importantly, won by the successful management of the broad spectrum of sociological complexities with a Whole of Government approach—rings equally true.

In 1999, two Chinese People's Liberation Army Colonels published an acclaimed book, *Unrestricted Warfare*. In *Unrestricted Warfare*, Senior Colonels Qiao Liang and Wang Xiangsui argued that in the globalized age of integrated and interdependent economies linked by "real time" media coverage, the face of war and the weapons of war have evolved beyond their traditional concepts. Advocating the use of unconventional strategies as the "new classic of war" for the 21st Century, Qiao and Wang argued that warfare has evolved beyond its traditional paradigm of the clash of professional soldier; the "blood and iron warrior" no longer had the monopoly on war. In the age of the "global village," the computer hacker, the "nonprofessional soldiers" such as the terrorist and guerrilla, the media mogul, the financier, the stock speculator, and indeed the ordinary media-consuming and voting citizen, have all become participants in warfare.* Qiao and Wang stated:

"War is no longer even war, but rather coming to grips on the internet and matching the mass media, assault and defence in forward exchange transactions, along with other things we never viewed as war....we need to be ascertaining a new type of fighting method within various uncertainties. It should not be that single type of prescription for treating the symptom and not the disease, but rather a hybrid type of learning widely from

---

* Lowe (2004) p30

strong points of others and gathering advantages as to allow a pear tree to bear both pears and apples."*

Qiao and Wang advocated a unified "grand warfare method" combining all aspects of military and civil fields and sweeping away the paradigm of traditional "force on force" war. These include, but are not limited to concepts such as terrorist war; financial war through financial market manipulation; economic war through the provision of economic aid, smuggling, and drug trafficking; public opinion war through the manipulation of media and information; ecological war by the manipulation of the environment; information war through the attacks on critical information infrastructure.†

However whilst the Unrestricted Warfare concept was touted as a "new classic of warfare," both in China and in the West, its fundamental premises, that is that conflict is an act of holistic statecraft, involving all functions of state, be they military, civil, or anthropological, lies with the "old classics" of Chinese strategic thought. The precepts contained within the classics of Chinese strategic thought are holistic in nature and regard war, peace, strategy, and diplomacy as parts of a greater continuum of statecraft, rather than as discrete and merely interlinked components of state. Consequently, the socio-political complexity of the 21st century conflict environment, especially that of counterinsurgency, cannot be navigated or approached with a rationalist, scientific method or via the rigidity of doctrinal dogma. T.E. Lawrence in reflecting on the Arab Revolt in *Seven Pillars of Wisdom*, noted that the "Turks were stupid; the Germans behind them dogmatical. They would believe that rebellion was absolute like war, and deal with it on the analogy of war." War, particularly counterinsurgency in the 21st century, like the counterinsurgencies and wars of imperial policing, can

---

* Qiao Liang and Wang Xiangsui. *Chaoxian Zhan — dui quanqiuhua shidai zhanzheng yu zhanfa de xiangding. (Unrestricted Warfare — Thoughts on Warfare and Strategy in the Globalized Era.) Jiefangjun Wenyi Chubanshe, Beijing* (Liberation Army Arts Publishing House, Beijing) 1999 p141.

† *Ibid*, p119.

not be neatly or successfully conducted through the application of firepower or technology, nor can it be won through the notion of absolute victory on the battlefield. Counterinsurgency or "war on rebellion" is, as Lawrence famously put it, "messy and slow, like eating soup with a knife."* It demands a flexible and adaptive approach, requiring an understanding of the ever dynamic relationships of the socio-political, physical and technological complex. It demands the understanding that war is a complex sociological problem, which demands complex sociological solutions.† It demands a contemplative approach, by which these complexities and their interrelationships are recognized, so that actions can be intuited in order to optimize the strategic effects. In short, the practise of postmodern warfare requires the pre-modern classical Chinese understanding and approach. It requires the classical notion of a unified practitioner of statecraft, which due to the immediacy and connectivity of the modern world, has been compressed from the level of ministers and generals, to that of the junior leader in the field: the strategic corporal.

Indeed, the awareness of the importance of Chinese strategic thought in the present day is such that, just before Christmas 2002 in the run up to the Iraq war, *Sun Tzu* was among the 100,000 books issued to the waiting troops by the US Army.‡ Whether Western strategists, generals, and soldiers understand the fundamental philosophies and concepts contained in Chinese strategic thought and are able apply them *in their entirety and in context* is itself another matter. Given the descent into civil-military chaos in Iraq following the invasion and after the elections of 2005, it appears that this is unlikely. "Despite the

---

* T.E. Lawrence, *Seven Pillars of Wisdom. A triumph.* (Jonathan Cape, London), 5th ed 1936 p193. Lawrence's statement has been most recently made famous by John Nagl. See John A. Nagl, *Counterinsurgency Lessons from Malaya and Vietnam. Learning to Eat Soup with a Knife.* (Praeger, Westport) 2002.

† See Nagl 2002 for a comprehensive and comparative treatise on the nature of institutional and organizational culture in the British and US armies, and their respective approaches to the counterinsurgencies in Malaya and Vietnam.

‡ Coker (2003)

maturation of cultural awareness and knowledge in the Western strategic world, the question of whether this has been, or indeed ever will be applied in an 'overarching strategic framework,' with a 'Whole of Government approach' beyond counterinsurgency remains to be seen."* Until such a time that the true nature of the precepts of Chinese strategic thought can be not only appreciated and understood in their entirety, but also applied in the same manner, Chinese strategic writings will remain simply "fortune cookie wisdom" found as quotes at the beginning of chapters, or selectively quoted and applied, out of context.

So while it is now clear just how important classical Chinese strategic thought is in the 21ˢᵗ Century, in light of the explosion of the Sun Tzu cottage industry the question becomes "why do we need a reprint of this early translation of Sun Tzu and, for that matter, the other classic texts in Sadler's *The Chinese Martial Code?"*

In order to answer this question, we need to turn to the translator and author, Arthur Lindsay Sadler, to gain a true appreciation for his scholarship as a Japanologist, and by extension, his prescience of thought in the application of fundamental cultural knowledge to strategic culture and warfare.

Arthur Sadler's Translation

Amid the proliferation of translations and interpretations of Chinese strategic texts in the second half of the 20th Century, Arthur Lindsay Sadler's little known publication is a landmark in both translation and in the modern understanding of strategic thought. In translating and interpreting these three texts, *The Art of War of Sun Tzu, The Precepts of War by Sima Rangju,* and *Wu Zi on the Art of War*, Sadler published perhaps the earliest translations into English of the *Sima Fa* and *Wu Zi* texts.

---

* Shelia Miyoshi Jager, *On The Uses of Cultural Knowledge.* (Strategic Studies Institute, US Army War College, Carlise PA) 2007 p.v.

Sadler's translation of *Sun Tzu* is preceded only by three other translators. The first translation into English of *Sun Tzu* was by Captain E.F. Calthrop R.F.A. in 1905. A British Army student of Japanese language in Toyko, Calthrop translated a Japanese version of the text, which was published in Toyko as *Sonshi.** Calthrop followed in 1908 with *The Book of War, The Military Classic of the Far East*, a revision of his earlier 1905 work. Sadler states in his introduction to *Three Military Classics of China* that Calthrop's 1908 version is the only English translation of *Sun Tzu* that he had seen, and which he describes, with his characteristic generosity, as "somewhat in need of revision perhaps." Perhaps the definitive translation of *Sun Tzu* in the first half of the 20th Century, is the scholarly work in 1910 of the eminent Sinologist, Lionel Giles, *Sun Tzu on The Art of War. The Oldest Military Treatise in the World. Translated from the Chinese with introduction and critical notes*. In contrast to Sadler's gentlemanly critique, Giles was scathing of both of Calthrop's versions and acidly criticised Calthrop's work, which he described as "particularly bad".† A contemporary version is the less than satisfactory translation by E. Machell-Cox, *The Principles of War by Sun Tzu*, published in Ceylon by the Royal Air Force in 1943.

Beyond Sadler's version of *Sun Tzu*, his translations of the *Sima Fa* and *Wu Zi* may well be the first translations of these texts into English. Certainly Samuel B. Griffith's 1963 landmark translation of *Sun Tzu*, appended by his translation of *Wu Zi* makes no reference to any preceding versions beyond Sadler's *Three Military Classics of China*.‡

Of his own translation, Sadler states: "Since these works are archaic and often concise even to ambiguity, and this applies particularly to Sima Rangju, it is not always easy to determine

* Sonshi being Japanese for Sunzi. Lionel Giles, *Sun Tzu on The Art of War. The Oldest Military Treatise in the World. Translated from the Chinese with introduction and critical notes* by Lionel Giles. (Luzac & Co, London) 1910 pVIII.
† *Ibid.*
‡ Griffith (1963) pp151-168, p183.

their meaning or to choose between the various suggestions of the commentators. Much of it must therefore be regarded as but tentative." Much of the difficulty of translating classical Chinese texts lies within the classical Chinese written language itself, in which the monosyllabic words may have different meanings and where meaning and nuance can often only be determined by the grammatical arrangement. Consequently, classical Chinese texts rely heavily on semantic meaning to convey nuance and subtext, which assumed that the contemporary reader was familiar with a wider corpus of literary scholarship of the day. There is little literary distinction between the great strategic texts and the great "philosophical" texts of the period. The classical strategic texts are not simply dry and unimaginative military field manuals, intended to be read by an unimaginative, soldierly mind. Above all else, China was and remains a literary society. The classical thinkers, including the great strategists, were literati and scholars of the highest caliber. Those who first recorded and compiled their thoughts and words, were not mere scribes, but also scholars, as were intended readers; the rulers, ministers, and generals. Their writings are eloquent in literary style, full of the use of imagery, allegory, and metaphor as befitting their place in the literary corpus. Although conceptual expression in classical Chinese is difficult due limitations in the language, paradoxically its inherent terseness and brevity produces a natural rhyme and meter. The natural and distinctive poetic cadence of classical Chinese, even in military texts gives them a natural aesthetic that lends itself very well to the gravity of the subject matter. Some of this gravity is lost to some degree in translation, and what is profound and beautiful in classical Chinese, becomes somewhat matter-of-fact or (overly) simplistic in English. This is particularly true of the *Sun Tzu*, which conveys concepts of abstract reality at a much higher level than the much more practical matter of the *Sima Fa* and the *Wu Zi*.

We do not know what versions of the original Chinese texts or commentaries that Sadler may have had, beyond the Chinese text of the *Wu Zi* published in the 1944 edition. Certainly, being an expert on Japanese feudal lords and samurai, Sadler may well have had an extensive collection of the classical Chinese texts via the Japanese warrior-literati and their associated commentaries to guide his translations. Even so, Sadler's text contains some remarkably imprecise translation of some critically important cultural terms, pertaining to some of the most fundamental concepts of Chinese thought, such as the *Dao* (the "Way"), virtue, and benevolence (as Confucian concepts), which significantly change the nuances and meanings of the text. However to be fair, we must recognise that the average intelligent reader of 1944 may have been much less familiar with such basic concepts of Chinese thought than the average modern reader. Therefore, we can afford to be kinder to Sadler's sometimes less than precise translations. We should make allowances for the fact that he was translating these texts hurriedly under wartime conditions, in competition with the parallel demands of teaching and perhaps secret war work. We should also allow for the fact that perhaps Sadler was rendering terminology and philosophical and socio-political concepts of Spring and Autumn Period China into more readable and easily understood terms for the reader of 1944. In his work on this pioneering translation, Sadler, unlike subsequent translators, certainly lacked access to the wide body of scholarship that exists today in English. We do not know what sources of scholarship Sadler may have had either in Chinese or Japanese to guide his translation, although it may be a reasonable assumption that resources were available to him. Certainly, it is clear that he relied on Sima Qian's *Shiji* as a source of biographical information. For the benefit of clarity of the much better informed modern reader, whenever Sadler's less than satisfactory translations have been found, they have been retranslated from the original Chinese texts in order to distil their true meaning and are noted appropriately.

That being said, Sadler's translations remain to this day eminently readable to the non-specialist, without the philosophical and political *obscuranta* of the terminology of Spring and Autumn Period China.

Of the adversities of scholarship in wartime, Sadler was particularly lucky in working as he was, in the comparative safety of Sydney. We must spare a thought for Sadler's contemporary translator of the *Sun Tzu*, Edward Machell-Cox, whose *The Principles of War by Sun Tzu* (RAF, Ceylon 1943) contained the poignant apology to the reader for the "defects" in translation, owing to the loss of most of the materials assembled for the purpose of his book, due to the Japanese attack!* Additionally, Machell-Cox also states that the translation was also delayed by the attack, due to his energies being directed in "other channels." This is perhaps to be expected, as he was after all, Squadron Leader Machell-Cox of the Royal Air Force![†] Of Arthur Sadler's war time role and possible war work, more remains to be discovered.

Arthur Sadler's Commentary

In 1944 at a time of a global, industrialized, total war conducted largely through the prism of the strategic and tactical legacies of European strategists such as Antoine-Henri Jomini and Carl von Clausewitz, Sadler's commentary to his translations on "the true Chinese view of militarism" perhaps makes the first commentary in English on what is today understood as "strategic culture." Commenting on the distinctiveness of the Chinese concept of strategy and warfare as transmitted by the ancient philosopher-commanders in their texts, Sadler noted that in seeking the most "effective means of obtaining victory," they "quite evidently" regarded war as an unnecessary act of last resort; that they held an inherent aversion to unnecessary or excessive use of force; and that they did not "hesitate to

---

* E. Machell-Cox, *The Principles of War by Sun Tzu.* (Royal Air Force, Ceylon). 1943 pix.

† Chris Michaelides, *The William Dyce and Edward Machell Cox Collections of Art Sale Catalogues in the British Library.* (British Library) 2005 http://sherpa.bl.uk/29/01/salescataloguestalk.pdf.

caution the victor against all unnecessary destruction or harsh treatment of the vanquished."* Sadler noted also that the ancient philosopher-commanders understood that "He who conquers with the fewest battles is the best general and conciliatory treatment is the easiest way to subdue a province." In these observations, Sadler suggests that the ancient Chinese philosopher-commanders understood not only the continuum of politics and warfare, but much more critically, that they understood that politics and warfare were not simply polar opposite positions, but rather, they are much more intimately and dynamically connected. In contrast to the destruction of the war in 1944, the ancients understood that victory in war, with its inherent carnage and destruction was the less desired option, and that rather, wise and benevolent statecraft that could both achieve desired political outcomes and minimise suffering of friend and foe alike was in fact preferred.

In these brief commentaries Sadler drew possibly one of the earliest linkages between these principles found in the classic Chinese texts with thoughts on the conduct of strategy and conflict in the modern age, some forty years before the emergence of the notion and study of strategic culture. Indeed, Sadler noted "Here we have that incapacity to take militarism seriously that is so characteristic of the Chinese people, and that has been so great a factor in the unique persistence of their Empire and civilization." This represents a long precognitive echo of the simplest and most dominant view amongst contemporary strategic culturalists with even the most basic grasp of Chinese strategic thought; that is, the notion of the "antimilitarist" and "pacifist bias of the Chinese tradition."[†]

Critically, Sadler perhaps becomes the one of the earliest Western proponents of strategic culture and the recognition of

---

* Not only does this serve as a poignant reminder of the level of destruction and the nature of the industrial scale of the total war of 1944, but perhaps presciently described the remarkable peace and reconstruction of Europe and Japan at the end of the Second World War.

† Mott & Kim (2006) p3.

the distinctiveness of Chinese strategic thought. Remarking in his introduction to the book, Sadler noted: "The writings of these strategists have not only been regarded as authoritative by their own countrymen, but have also been carefully studied and followed by the Japanese military experts ever since medieval times, and are much quoted in their writings."

Essentially, Sadler suggests that since these texts are venerated and studied by the Japanese military leadership, they must be read and understood at the fundamental level, in order to engage and fight the Japanese effectively. In essence Sadler, the expert Orientalist, was expounding the greatest of the maxims of Chinese strategic thought—"know your enemy." E. Machell-Cox, Sadler's contemporary fellow translator of the *Sun Tzu*, and despite his less than satisfactory version of the text, is even more explicit: "Sun Tzu is fundamental and, read with insight, lays bare the mental mechanism of our enemy. STUDY HIM AND STUDY HIM AGAIN. Do not be misled by his simplicity. STUDY HIM, REFLECT UPON HIM, STUDY HIM AGAIN."*

Thus in 1944 at the height of the greatest of the "modernist" wars, decades before the birth of the study of strategic culture, Sadler, the Orientalist and by definition a culturalist, demonstrated remarkable prescience and clarity in articulating a remarkably contemporary view of "postmodern war." That is the contemporary notion that in warfare it is necessary to know the "cultural other"—that it is necessary to know the enemy, at a deep and fundamental level of cultural knowledge and "ethnography," in order to understand how and why he fights, and how to fight him effectively.

---

* Machell-Cox (1943) pvii.

Arthur Lindsay Sadler

Arthur Lindsay Sadler was born in 1882 at Hackney, London and was educated at Dulwich College, Merchant Taylor's School and St. John's College, Oxford (BA 1908, MA 1911) where he graduated with second class honors in Oriental languages (Hebrew and Assyrian).[*] At Oxford, Sadler became acquainted with Professor E.S. Morse's pioneering work on Japanese architecture, which undoubtedly influenced him in working and studying in Japan.[†] In 1908–1918, Sadler taught English and Latin at the Sixth Higher School, Okayama, and English at Peers' College, Tokyo (1918-1921). Sadler married Eva Botan Seymour, an Anglo-Japanese in 1916, and was council member of the Asiatic Society of Japan and appointed companion of the 5th Order of the Rising Sun in 1919.

Appointed as Professor of Oriental Studies at the University of Sydney in 1922, Sadler expanded the curriculum in oriental history and Japanese language. Reserved and dignified, Sadler was popular with both students and staff, cutting a memorable and dapper figure in English tweed and sporting a pince-nez as his "constant mode of dress."[‡] This however, belied a warm and affable nature, which saw Sadler and Mrs. Sadler extending invitations to his students to tea at his Sydney home, famous for its blend of European and Japanese aesthetics and complete with a Japanese tea house.[§] Avoiding university politics and administration, Sadler usually read during professorial board meetings. Rather, Sadler was well known at the university for his collections of Japanese and East Asian art

---

[*] Joyce Ackroyd, "Sadler, Arthur Lindsay (1882-1970)," *Australian Dictionary of Biography*, Online edition, (Australian National University) 2006 http://www.adb.online. anu.edu.au/biogs/A110514b.htm.

[†] Pamela Bell, "A. L. Sadler (1882-1970) Professor of Oriental Studies at the University of Sydney 1922-1947: His Ideas and Influence," in *Proceedings of the Pacific Rim Conference in Transcultural Aesthetics*. University of Sydney, June 18-20 1997, Eugenio Benitez (ed) p118.

[‡] Marsden Hordern, *A Merciful Journey. Recollections of a World War II Patrol Boat Man*. (The Miegunyah Press, Melbourne), 2005 p48.

[§] Marsden Hordern, (personal communication).

and artifacts, including a suit of Samurai armor in his office, as well as his practical expertise in the rituals of the Japanese tea ceremony and of Japanese swordsmanship. Sadler's expertise extended also to Japanese architecture and gardening—his Sydney home "Rivenhall" was famous at the time for Sadler's pioneering work in transcultural décor and landscape gardening. The house itself blended Neo-Georgian, Tudor, and Japanese architectural elements with self styled Jacobean furniture (hand crafted in Japan) and Oriental arts. The garden mixed elements of Italianate water features which complimented the ceremonial Japanese tea house and the Japanese styled well arch which disguised the vulgarity of the concrete septic tank; all set amongst the Japanese inspired landscaping designed and constructed by own hand.*

Sadler's university history course was available to non-language students and included the period of the Tokugawa Shogunate and an introduction to East Asian and Indian culture. His lectures were popular and well attended, filled with humorous anecdotes and quirky asides which students were to recall years later. By the same token, the intellectual content, with the emphasis on European contact in East Asia and that of European and Asian comparative history and culture was analytical and topical in the period between the wars, particularly amidst a growing consciousness of Japanese aggression and expansionism in Asia.† From 1931–1937, Sadler was concurrent Professor of Japanese at the Royal Military College of Australia, Sydney ("Duntroon Wing, Victoria Barracks"). At both institutions, Sadler's teaching was to have a preparatory note for the young men who would soon encounter the Japanese as an enemy in the not too far distant future. When faced with the horrors of a brutal enemy, Sadler's former students such as Lieutenant Marsden Hordern RANR remembered clearly the "tragic truth

---

* Marsden Hordern, (personal communication).

† After C.D. Coulthard-Clark, *Duntroon. The Royal Military College of Australia, 1911-1986.* (Allen & Unwin, Sydney), 1986 p129; Ackroyd (1988); Bell (1997); Hordern (2005) p49, and M. Hordern, (personal communication).

of his words" from the lectures given by Sadler on the nature of the Japanese bushido mentality and ethic.*

Arthur Sadler was a noted scholar in the pre-modern style with an expertise in history, literature, art, philology, and antiquities. Sadler was extensively published in many fields with expertise designed to "give the intelligent non-specialist an insight into the Japanese mentality."† Sadler's list of books included topics in pre-modern and modern Japanese literature, Chinese classics, Japanese art and aesthetics, flower arranging and tea ceremony, and architecture. These include *The Ten Foot Square Hut & Tales of Heike* (1928), *The Art of Flower Arrangement in Japan* (1933), *Cha-No-Yu The Japanese Tea Ceremony* (1933), *Japanese Plays No-Kyogen-Katuki* (1934), *The Ise Daijinggu Sankikei: Or Diary of a Pilgrim to Ise* (1940), *Selections from Confucian Texts* (1942), and *Selection from Modern Japanese Writers* (1943). All of Sadler's publications in these fields represented some of the earliest transmission of these fields of endeavor into a wider audience in English.

Of particular note are his works at the nexus of culture and the fields of history and international relations, perhaps marking Sadler as one of the pioneering scholars of "strategic culture." These works include; The *Influence of Japanese Culture and Tradition on her Foreign Relations* (1935), "The Naval Campaign in the Korean War of Hideyoshi (1592-1598), *Transactions of the Asiatic Society of* Japan, 2.11 (1937), *The Maker of Modern Japan, the Life of Tokugawa Ieyasu* (1937), *Three Military Classics of China* (1944), and *A Short History of Japan* (1946 & 1962).

During World War II when Australia was heavily engaged in the South West Pacific theater against Japan, Arthur Sadler and Mrs. Sadler were subject to an unfortunate level of animosity, due to their Japanese connections.‡ Australian military intelligence files dated 1941–1943 on both Professor and Mrs.

---

* Hordern (2005) p49 & Marsden Hordern, (personal communication).
† D. 18573 Extract from *Sydney Morning Herald* June 16, 1993.
‡ Hordern, (personal communication)

Sadler reveal a significant intrusion into their privacy with unsubstantiated reports of disloyalty or subversion, in the period prior to and immediately after the Japanese hostilities against the British Empire in December 1941. Hysterical accusations of disloyalty, subversion, and "5th column" activities by anonymous sources based on secondhand information or reported by self appointed guardians of public security, none of whom seem to have been personally acquainted with the Sadlers, feature in the Sadlers' military intelligence files.[*] Most obviously, these accusations of "disloyalty" were cast on Mrs. Sadler by virtue of being considered "Japanese" (she was in fact a British subject and daughter of a Royal Navy officer) and on Professor Sadler by virtue of marriage and his "oriental mindedness." Repeated investigation by police and military intelligence throughout 1941 and 1942 determined that all accusations were completely unsubstantiated. Indeed, Mrs. Sadler seems to have been considered more reliable than her husband, on the basis of her entirely British upbringing, education, and benevolent activities in the local community. In fact, a May 1941 report by Lt. Newman of Intelligence Service General Staff, Eastern Command, states that: "She is a much stronger more incisive character than her husband, and could easily find out what work he was doing were she so inclined."[†]

Those who knew the Sadlers, such as their neighbors and Professor Sadler's colleagues and students, widely supposed that he was in some way involved in war work, perhaps in cryptography and code breaking or some other form of intelligence analysis.[‡] Sadler alluded to some possible involvement in his later correspondence with former student Marsden Hordern, and it has been suggested that Sadler's former student, Dr. M J Morrissey, himself a Japanese interpreter and intelligence officer during World War II, may have renewed his acquaintance

---

[*] NAA: Arthur Lindsay Sadler C123, 18573; NAA: Eva Botan Sadler. British Nee Seymour, C123 18608.

[†] *Ibid.*

[‡] Hordern, (personal communication).

with Sadler through their connection in military intelligence work.* Certainly Sadler's expertise was called upon for service as a translator in the Sydney Censor's Office until at least June 1941[†] and in 1942 Sadler advised the Australian government on the handling of the remains of Japanese submariners killed in the attack on Sydney Harbor.[‡] Military and police intelligence reports of 1941–1942 reveal that Sadler seems to have been subject of some suspicion in his duties as an official translator in the Sydney Censor's Office in March –June 1941, as a result of a less than rigorous approach to censorship.[§] This perhaps can be attributed to a degree of naiveté on his part, in terms of the consequences of anything other than a completely stringent approach to official duties. On one occasion, Sadler's clear position of professional academic neutrality in commentary and recommendation of action, in lieu of a more stringent commentary based on political realities or perhaps a more jingoistic attitude, cast further doubt on his loyalty and reliability. Further research is required to determine if Sadler was actually engaged in intelligence work after the commencement of war with Japan in December 1941, despite earlier suspicions. Sadler continued his scholarly work throughout the war and wrote articles in the *Sydney Morning Herald* on Japanese military culture in 1945.[¶]

In his translation of the classic texts of Chinese strategic thought, itself the root of the Japanese strategic culture, Sadler made an additional, if only minor and at the time, seemingly insignificant contribution to the war effort. While the publication of the *Three Military Classics of China* in 1944 was not an official government publication, the very fact that it was published at all, in a time of wartime austerity does suggest that a degree of importance was ascribed to this book. Trans-

---

* Hordern, (personal communication), Bell (1997) p116

† NAA: Arthur Lindsay Sadler C123, 18573; NAA: Eva Botan Sadler. British Nee Seymour, C123 18608

‡ Bell (1997) p125

§ Military Police Intelligence files, NAA: Arthur Lindsay Sadler C123, 18573; NAA: Eva Botan Sadler. British Nee Seymour, C123 18608.

¶ Bell (1997) p125

port difficulties and the restrictions of vital necessities for the war effort severely curtailed publishing and printing during the Second World War. Supplies of local and imported paper for the purposes of commercial publishing were controlled by the Australian government's Division of Import Procurement, while publishing and printing priorities were assessed in conjunction with the Book Sponsorship Committee. These government bodies determined that priority publishing items were school books and works of "national importance."* It can only be supposed that Sadler's *Three Military Classics of China*, along with his other wartime publications, were considered to be of "national importance" in their contribution to the war effort. Additionally, the fact that one of the most pre-eminent experts in Japanese was able to devote a significant effort in terms of valuable intellectual manpower towards its production is further indicative of the importance of this book.

Through his teaching and scholarship, Arthur Sadler clearly demonstrated that his deep and expert knowledge of Japanese history and culture provided him with a clear and intricate knowledge of the Japanese military ethic and institutional culture. Moreover, Sadler's intrinsic knowledge of "Japaneseness" at the most fundamental levels of culture, philosophy and literature, or in the modern parlance "ethnography," enabled him to understand the absolute imperative of transmitting this knowledge (of "knowing the enemy"—itself one of the fundamental axioms of the Japanese strategic mind), as the basis of the enemy's institutional and strategic culture. A quintessential Victorian Orientalist, with an expert scholarly and cultural knowledge, Sadler was the very essence of the British imperial adventure. That essence, which made the Victorian and post-Victorian British such experts in cultural and conflict ethnography, was the basis of their success in Imperial governance and policing. This in itself was the basis of the British success in

---

* Martyn Lyons, "The Book Trade and the Australian Reader in 1945" in *A History of the Book in Australia 1891–1945. A National Culture in a Colonised Market*. Martyn Lyons and John Arnold eds. (University of Queensland Press, St Lucia, 2001). p401.

the conduct of counterinsurgency operations throughout the height and into the decline of the British Empire, from as far a field as Malayan jungles to the streets of Northern Ireland.*

At a time, decades before the advent of the field of strategic culture, when classic Chinese strategic texts were nothing more than curiosities at the hands of philologists and Orientalists, and amidst the all consuming Leviathan of industrialised global war; when Clausewitzian and Jominian doctrine reigned supreme, the clarity of insight of Arthur L. Sadler and his intent in the transmission of this knowledge was nothing short of pioneering.

The Chinese Martial Code

The Chinese Martial Code, is a continuation of the two thousand year old living tradition of the Chinese art of warfare. Written by solider-scholars, these classic texts reflect the Chinese view of the world, and their vision of statecraft and strategy has left a distinctive legacy through the millennia which still resonate into the present day. Warfare in the 21st century may be on the surface, some two thousand years removed from the warfare of the Warring States and of bronze and iron age war. In the information age however, wars are still wars. Although weapons and tactics have changed beyond the wildest imagination of Sun Wu, Sima Rangju and Wu Qi, their fundamental wisdom of strategy, politics, knowledge, intuition, administration, and organization remain the same. The great masters of the Spring and Autumn Period and Warring States China would feel very much at home in the 21st Century, despite smart bombs and unmanned aerial vehicles. Indeed we can almost imagine these soldier-scholars standing shoulder to shoulder with their modern day counterparts engaged in the problems of insurgency and counterinsurgency in Iraq and Afghanistan.

---

* For detail, see Sir Charles W. Gwynn, *Imperial Policing*, Macmillan, London 1934; John A. Nagl, *Learning to Eat Soup with a Knife*: *Counterinsurgency Lessons from Malaya and Vietnam*, University of Chicago Press: Chicago, Ill. 2002.

The 1944 work of Professor Arthur Lindsay Sadler is a part of this tradition of scholarship in the Chinese art of war. Through Sadler's expert knowledge of East Asian culture and thought, we find in his work on the *Three Military Classics of China,* a significant and timely contribution to the corpus of scholarly work of the great Chinese strategists in the English language. Given the timing of this original work in the years before the wars in Korea and Indochina, we can only wonder at the impact it may have had, had it received a wider circulation and if the military leadership had not been blinded to the fundamental truths of war, by the efficacy of the technological marvels of the industrial age.

We are reminded of this peril by Sir Basil Liddell-Hart, the great British strategist of the 1920s and student of Sun Tzu.* An early advocate of mechanised and armored warfare, Liddell-Hart emphasised the strategy of "indirect approach," that is attacks on the line of least resistance; and the disruption of the enemy's equilibrium as being the key to victory. During the Second World War, Liddell-Hart was visited by the Chinese Military Attaché, a student of Chiang Kai-shek, who told him that his and J.F.C. Fuller's books (on mechanised warfare) were primary text books in the Chinese military academies.† Liddell-Hart asked: "What about Sun Tzu?" The officer replied that while it was "venerated as a classic, it was considered out of date by younger officers and thus hardly worth study in the era of mechanised weapons." To this Liddell-Hart suggested that they revisit Sun Tzu, since that "one small book contained as much about the fundamentals of strategy and tactics as I had covered in more than twenty books."‡

In 1949, Chiang Kai-shek's Kuomintang army, well armed and equipped with Western weapons was defeated in the civil war by the People's Liberation Army, led by Mao Zedong. Clearly Liddell-Hart's advice was not considered, nor did Chiang

---

* Presumably via Lionel Giles' 1910 version of *Sun Tzu.*

† B.H. Liddell-Hart, "Foreward" in Griffith 1963, *Ibid* p.vii.

‡ *Ibid.*

Kai-shek's officers "know their enemy, and know themselves."
Like Liddell-Hart, Mao was a student of Sun Tzu, whose work
he considered "scientific truths."* Teaching Sun Tzu's fundamental strategies at the Red Army University in Yanan, the PLA
implemented these fundamentals through Mao's strategies of
guerrilla and mobile warfare, against the Kuomintang in the
civil war, and then against the United States in Korea. In turn
Võ Nguyên Giáp, student of Sun Tzu and Mao Zedong, raised
these "scientific truths" to their zenith, first to humiliate France
and later the United States in the wars in Indochina.

In the 21st Century, war and conflict remains an essential part
of the human condition. When faced with the challenges of
strategy and security, be it Iraq, Afghanistan, Iran, or contemplating the "Rising China," we must be reminded of perhaps
the least remembered, but most important of all of the maxims of Chinese strategic thought: "A ruler can not mobilise his
armies in anger. A general can not engage in battle in wrath....
Anger can revert to joy, wrath can revert to delight, but a nation
in ruins can not be restored, and the dead can not be brought
back to life."†

Edwin H. Lowe
Sydney 2008

---

* Zhang Shuguang, *Mao's Military Romanticism. China and the Korean War 1950-
1953.* University of Kansas Press, 1995 pp20-22.

† Translated from *Sunzi Bingfa* chapter 13, Yin Que Shan text, in Ames (1993) p164.

Introduction

THE authors of these three works were contemporaries of the well-known ethical teachers Confucius and Mencius, for they wrote in the 6th, 5th, and 4th centuries B.C. respectively. They were practical and successful soldiers as well as authors, and they lived in days when there were plenty of opportunities for their talents. From 1122 to 225 B.C. the Empire was ruled by the great Zhou dynasty* with its record of nearly a thousand years of sovereignty; but though in theory the Zhou Emperor was supreme in the "under heaven," actually he soon ceased to have much authority, which was usurped by a "Protector" who was the most powerful of the feudal lords of the various states, and who tried to keep the rest in order.† It was a condition that was later to be imitated by the Shoguns of medieval Japan. But as these feudal lords became practically independent, each strove to maintain his power or improve it by attacking his neighbor and continual hostilities were the unfortunate result. Naturally such diademed banditti valued professors of the military art more than ethical teachers, so that even Confucius was asked if he could give instruction in tactics by the Duke Ding, of his state of Lu, to which he replied acidly that what he knew how to handle were not companies of soldiers but sacrificial vessels. The laughing comment of the crowd, "Virtue in a back seat and strumpetry to the fore," that greeted the sage when he had perforce to ride behind the carriage of the Duke Ling of Wei and his notorious concubine, satirizes the unethical tendencies of feudal lords, as the sharp comment of Mencius that a man

---

* The Chinese state is not considered to be regarded as an "empire" until 221BCE, when the Warring States were unified by force under the First Emperor of the Qin Dynasty.

† The Zhou Emperor should be correctly considered the Zhou King.

who prided himself on his skill in war was just a great criminal well expresses the true Chinese view of militarism.

And it is clear that these experts in strategy, though they are practical enough in describing what they considered the most effective means of obtaining victory, quite evidently regard war as only an unfortunate necessity that followed on the very unideal temperaments of these feudal rulers, and neither disguise its evil effects on the peasants who have to fight it, nor hesitate to caution the victor against all unecessary destruction or harsh treatment of the vanquished. It was a misfortune which the ancients in their wisdom and benevolence were able to dispense with. He who conquers with the fewest battles is the best general and conciliatory treatment is the easiest way to subdue a province. Here we have that incapacity to take militarism seriously that is so characteristic of the Chinese people, and that has been so great a factor in the unique persistence of their Empire and civilization.

The earliest of these writers, Sun Tzu, of the late 6th century, with his near contemporary Sima Rangju, apparently antedate the first Greek military author, Aeneas Tacticus, whose work is conjectured to belong to the middle of the 4th century B.C., and who would be, therefore, of about the same era as the Chinese Wu Qi. Incidentally rather less seems to be known of Aeneas than of the Chinese tacticians, little though that is. Neither do they discuss the same type of problem, for the Greek strategist has most to say about strongholds and sieges, the last thing a wise general engages in according to the Chinese view.

All these Chinese writers were practical men and leaders of the armies of the feudal chiefs of their day. Sun Tzu was in the service of Helü, King of Wu (reigned 514-496 B.C.), a state lying on each side of the Yangzi to the east of Chu and north of Yue, with its capital near the modern Suzhou. Under this ruler began the wars between Wu and Yue that have made their names proverbial ever since as quarrelsome neighbors. Little is known of Sun Tzu except that he was a man of Qi, and the oft-repeated story that he drilled the king's women in two regiments at his request and cut off the heads of the two leaders, his favorite concubines, because they did not take him seriously. After which all went very well.* It is said that he led an army of 30,000 of the Wu troops and defeated one of 200,000 from Chu. It is also stated that he wrote eighty-two volumes, only thirteen of which have survived, and that there were writers on military subjects before him, but all their work has perished.

---

* This episode is recounted by Sima Qian, the Grand Historian of the Han Dynasty (145-86 BCE) in his monumental historiography of China from the legendary Yellow Emperor, Huangdi to the reign of Emperor Wudi of Han. This episode is perhaps the most famous "job interview" in history. On being granted an audience with King Helü of Wu, who had read the *Art of War*, Sun Tzu was asked by the King if he could turn the ladies of the palace into a troop of soldiers. One hundred and eighty ladies were formed into two companies, with the King's favorites appointed as company commanders. Sun Tzu asked the ladies if they knew their front from back and left from right. Assured that they did, Sun Tzu instructed them twice on the orders for advance, left turn, right turn and retire, after which the ladies assured him that they had understood. When Sun Tzu gave the drum signal, followed by the order "Right Turn," the ladies burst into laughter. Sun Tzu said "If the rules are not clear and orders are not understood, the commander is to blame." Sun Tzu then repeated the instructions a third and fourth time, after which he gave the drum signal and ordered "Left Turn." Again, the ladies burst into laughter. Sun Tzu said "If the rules are not clear and orders are not understood, the commander is to blame. But when orders are clear yet not carried out, it is the officers who are to blame." Sun Tzu prepared to execute the company commanders, at which the King gave the instruction that his two favorite ladies be spared. Despite the King's protestations, Sun Tzu executed the ladies saying "I have been appointed commander and a general in the field is not bound by orders from his sovereign." Sun Tzu appointed two new commanders and after which, when the signals were again given, the ladies executed their orders precisely. King Helü was invited to inspect his new troops with a message from Sun Tzu saying "The troops are in fighting order, ready for inspection. Your Majesty can do what you please with them—they will go through fire or water." The King declined, at which Sun Tzu said "Your majesty is only interested in theory, not the real thing." After Sima Qian, "Sun Zi Wu Qi liezhuan" *Shiji*. ("Sun Zi and Wu Qi. Biographies", *The Records of the Grand Historian*), vol 65. 109 BC to 91 BC.

While on the surface, Sun Tzu's reply "I have been appointed commander and a general in the field is not bound by orders from his sovereign" may perhaps suggests a primacy of the military over the civil government, this is certainly not the case. Sun Tzu is actually suggesting that political interference after the army has been deployed is folly and that once troops have been deployed in the field the commander should be free of the interference from the civil government. However, a reading of Sun Tzu reveals that Sun Tzu is of course not a militarist by any means. Throughout *The Art of War*, Sun Tzu states that the use of armed force should only be after careful deliberation, and even then, it is the last resort when all other strategies of statecraft have been exhausted. Sun Tzu in effect suggests that the aims and objectives of conflict, both strategic and political in a unified and holistic manner must be clearly defined and understood by both the civil and military leadership *before* the commitment of the use of force. However once the forces have been deployed to the field, political interference from the civil leadership should not be tolerated. Sima Rangju clearly states this in his book as well, in Chapter 1 "Concerning the Heavenly Sovereign."

Sima Rangju seems to have lived a little later, and to have been in the service of the Duke Jing of Qi which lay next to the state of Lu, the home of Confucius. The Duke Jing had no use for this sage, who stayed in Qi for two years hoping to be put in charge of its administration. As he was not, he went back to Lu and became an official there and brought about such order that the Duke Jing became alarmed at the possibilities of such efficiency, so that he sent to the Duke of Lu a present of a hundred and twenty horses and eighty female musicians to distract his attention from too much austere planning. In this he was successful enough, but he might have been more so at much less expense had he employed the sage himself, beside achieving certain posthumous fame. Instead he appointed Rangju to lead his armies, which he did so efficiently that he gained much honor and the title of *Da Sima* or President of the Board of War.* He was eventually dismissed, however, owing to the slanders of another minister and died shortly afterwards.

Of Wu Qi rather more is related. He came from Wei and studied with one of the disciples of Confucius named Zeng Shen, but his master took a dislike to him and sent him away.†

He then went to Lu and became a specialist in the military art, and had hopes of being put in command of the state forces. But his wife was from Qi, the enemy with which Lu was contending, and the Prince therefore hesitated. This being the only obstacle apparent Wu Qi disposed of it quite simply by putting his wife to death and got the post. Then he went to Wei, where we find him in the treatise in the service of the Marquis Wu (386-371 B.C.).‡ It seems that potentate asked Li Ke, one of his

---

* "Minister of War" is more appropriate.

† Zeng Shen, also known as Zeng Zi (Master Zeng). Zeng Zi severed relations with Wu Qi after he failed to observe the mourning rites when his mother died—a great offence in the Confucian tradition. See also the general Introduction additional biographical information.

‡ Prior to Marquis Wu of Wei, Wu Qi served his father, the Marquis Wen (403-387 BCE). Marquis Wen instituted sweeping reforms to the state of Wei, using the methods from a variety of teachers and traditions. Sima Qian, "*Wei Ce Jin*" ("The House of Wei") *Shiji*, (*The Records of the Grand Historian*) vol 44. 109-91 BCE. Zhonghua Publishing House, Beijing 1959.

ministers, what sort of a man Wu was, and he replied: "He is greedy and fond of women, but in handling troops even Sima Rangju is not superior." The Lu forces did well under him, but after a while he failed to be appreciated and fled to Chu, where he was again a successful disciplinarian and leader. Though he was popular with the troops because he shared all their hardships, "sleeping on the ground without a mat and carrying his rations like a common soldier," he was disliked by the officials for his strictness and correction of abuses by which they profited. So on the death of the King of Chu he was put to death by the new ruler in 381 B.C. at the age of seventy.

The writings of these strategists have not only been regarded as authoritative by their own countrymen, but have also been carefully studied and followed by the Japanese military experts ever since medieval times, and are much quoted in their writings. They seem originally to have been kept as a secret teaching by these professors who were salaried as advisers of the feudal lords. The only English version of any of them that I have seen is that of E. F. Calthrop, a translation of Sun Tzu entitled "The Book of War, a military classic of the Far East," 1908, long out of print and somewhat in need of revision perhaps. Since these works are archaic and often concise even to ambiguity, and this applies particularly to Sima Rangju, it is not always easy to determine their meaning or to choose between the various suggestions of the commentators. Much of it must therefore be regarded as but tentative.

The appended Chinese text of Wu Qi may perhaps be useful to students of the language who wish to sample a work of this kind. No one is more conscious of the regrettable calligraphy than the author, but it is to be hoped that it will at least be found legible.

A.L.S.
Sydney, 1944.

The Art of War of Sun Tzu
(CHINESE TEXT)
孫 子 兵 法

計篇第一

孫子曰：兵者，國之大事。死生之地，存亡之道，不可不察也。故經之以五，校之以計，而索其情：一曰道，二曰天，三曰地，四曰將，五曰法。道者，令民與上同意也。故可與之死，可與之生，而民不畏危。天者，陰陽、寒暑、時制也。地者，遠近、險易、廣狹、死生也。將者，智、信、仁、勇、嚴也。法者，曲制、官道、主用也。凡此五者，將莫不聞，知之者勝，不知之者不勝。故校之以計，而索其情。曰：主孰有道？將孰有能？天地孰得？法令孰行？兵眾孰強？士卒孰練？賞罰孰明？吾以此知勝負矣。

將聽吾計，用之必勝，留之；將不聽吾計，用之必敗，去之。計利以聽，乃為之勢，以佐其外。勢者，因利而制權也。兵者，詭道也。故能而示之不能，用而示之不用，近而示之遠，遠而示之近。利而誘之，亂而取之，實而備之，強而避之。怒而撓之，卑而驕之，佚而勞之，親而離之，攻其無備，出其不意。此兵家之勝，不可先傳也。夫未戰而廟算勝者，得算多也；未戰而廟算不勝者，得算少也。多算勝，少算不勝，而況無算乎！吾以此觀之，勝負見矣。

作戰篇第二

孫子曰：凡用兵之法，馳車千駟，革車千乘，帶甲十萬，千里饋糧，則內外之費，賓客之用，膠漆之材，車甲之奉，日費千金，然後十萬之師舉矣。其用戰也勝久則鈍兵挫銳，攻城則力屈，久暴師則國用不足。夫鈍兵挫銳，屈力殫貨，則諸侯乘其弊而起，雖有智者，不能善其後矣。故兵聞拙速，未睹巧之久也。夫兵久而國利者，未之有也。故不盡知用兵之害者，則不能盡知用兵之利也。善用兵者，役不再籍，糧不三載；取用於國，因糧於敵，故軍食可足也。國之貧於師者遠輸，遠輸則百姓貧。近於師者貴賣，貴賣則百姓財竭，財竭則急於丘役。力屈、財殫，中原內虛於家。百姓之費，十去其七。

公家之費：破軍罷馬，甲冑矢弩，戟楯蔽櫓，丘牛大車，十去其六。故智將務食于敵。食敵一鐘，當吾二十鐘；蕋稈一石，當吾二十石。故殺敵者，怒也；取敵之利者，貨也。故車戰，得車十乘已上，賞其先得者，而更其旌旗，車雜而乘之，卒善而養之，是謂勝敵而益強。故兵貴勝，不貴久。故知兵之將，民之司命，國家安危之主也。

謀攻篇第三

孫子曰：凡用兵之法，全國為上，破國次之；全軍為上，破軍次之。全旅為上，破旅次之；全卒為上，破卒次之；全伍為上，破伍次之。是故百戰百勝，非善之善者也；不戰而屈人之兵，善之善者也。故上兵伐謀，其次伐交，其次伐兵，下政攻城。攻城之法為不得已。修櫓轒轀、具器械、三月而後成，距闉，又三月而後已。將不勝其忿，而蟻附之，殺士三分之一，而城不拔者，此攻之災也。故善用兵者，屈人之兵而非戰也。拔人之城而非攻也，毀人之國而非久也。必以全爭于天下，故兵不頓，而利可全，此謀攻之法也。

故用兵之法，十則圍之，五則攻之，倍則分之，敵則能戰之，少則能逃之，不若則能避之。故小敵之堅，大敵之擒也。

夫將者，國之輔也。輔周則國必強，輔隙則國必弱。故君之所以患于軍者三：不知軍之不可以進而謂之進，不知軍之不可以退而謂之退，是為縻軍；不知三軍之事，而同三軍之政者，則軍士惑矣；不知三軍之權，而同三軍之任，則軍士疑矣。三軍既惑且疑，則諸侯之難至矣，是謂亂軍引勝。

故知勝有五：知可以戰與不可以戰者勝，識眾寡之用者勝，上下同欲者勝，以虞待不虞者勝，將能而君不御者勝。此五者，知勝之道也。

故曰：知己知彼，百戰不殆；不知彼而知己，一勝一負；不知彼不知己，每戰必殆。

形篇第四

孫子曰：昔之善戰者，先為不可勝，以待敵之可勝。不可勝在己，可勝在敵。故善戰者，能為不可勝，不能使敵必可勝。故曰：勝可知，而不可為。

不可勝者，守也；可勝者，攻也。守則不足，攻則有餘。善守者，藏于九地之下；善攻者，動于九天之上。故能自保而全勝也。見勝不過眾人之所知，非善之善者也；戰勝而天下曰善，非善之善者也。故舉秋毫不為多力，見日月不為明目，聞雷霆不為聰耳。古之所謂善戰者，勝勝易勝者也。故善戰之勝也，無智名，無勇功。故其戰勝不忒。不忒者，其所措必勝，勝已敗者也。故善戰者，立於不敗之地，而不失敵之敗也。是故勝兵先

勝而後求戰，敗兵先戰而後求勝。善用兵者，修道而保
法，故能為勝敗之政。

　　兵法：一曰度，二曰量，三曰數，四曰稱，五曰勝。

　　地生度，度生量，量生數，數生稱，稱生勝。故勝兵
若以鎰稱銖，敗兵若以銖稱鎰。勝者之戰民也，若決積
水於千仞之谿者，形也。

執篇第五

孫子曰：凡治眾如治寡，分數是也；鬥眾如鬥寡，形名
是也；三軍之眾，可使必受敵而無敗者，奇正是也；兵
之所加，如以碬投卵者，虛實是也。

　　凡戰者，以正合，以奇勝。故善出奇者，無窮如天
地，不竭如江河。終而復始，日月是也。死而復生，四
時是也。聲不過五，五聲之變，不可勝聽也。色不過
五，五色之變，不可勝觀也。味不過五，五味之變，不
可勝嘗也。戰勢不過奇正，奇正之變，不可勝窮也。奇
正相生，如循環之無端，孰能窮之？激水之疾，至於
漂石者，勢也；鷙鳥之疾，至於毀拆者，節也。是故善
戰者，其勢險，其節短。勢如彍弩，節如發機。紛紛紜
紜，鬥亂而不可亂也。渾渾沌沌，形圓而不可敗也。亂
生于治，怯生于勇，弱生于強。治亂，數也；勇怯勢也；
強弱，形也。故善動敵者，形之，敵必從之；予之，敵
必取之。

　　以利動之，以卒待之。故善戰者，求之於勢，不責於
人，故能擇人而任勢。

　　任勢者，其戰人也，如轉木石。木石之性，安則靜，
危則動，方則止，圓則行。故善戰人之勢，如轉圓石於
千仞之山者，勢也。

虛實篇第六

孫子曰：凡先處戰地而待敵者佚，後處戰地而趨戰者勞。故善戰者，致人而不致於人。能使敵人自至者，利之也；能使敵人不得至者，害之也。故敵佚能勞之，飽能飢之，安能動之。出其所不趨，趨其所不意。行千里而不勞者，行於無人之地也。攻而必取者，攻其所不守也。守而必固者，守其所不攻也。故善攻者，敵不知其所守。善守者，敵不知其所攻。

微乎微乎，至於無形，神乎神乎，至於無聲，故能為敵之司命。進而不可禦者，衝其虛也；退而不可追者，速而不可及也。故我欲戰，敵雖高壘深溝，不得不與我戰者，攻其所必救也。我不欲戰，畫地而守之，敵不得與我戰者，乖其所之也。故形人而我無形，則我專而敵分；我專為一，敵分為十，是以十攻其一也，則我眾而敵寡；能以眾擊寡者，則吾之所與戰者，約矣。吾所與戰之地不可知，不可知，則敵所備者多，敵所備者多，則吾之所戰者，寡矣。故備前則後寡，備後則前寡，備左則右寡，備右則左寡，無所不備，則無所不寡。寡者備人者也，眾者使人備己者也。故知戰之地，知戰之日，則可千里而會戰。不知戰地，不知戰日，則左不能救右，右不能救左，前不能救後，後不能救前，而況遠者數十里，近者數里乎？

以吾度之，越人之兵雖多，亦奚益於勝敗哉。故曰：勝可為也。敵雖眾，可使無鬥。故策之而知得失之計。作之而知動靜之理，形之而知死生之地，角之而知有餘不足之處。故形兵之極，至於無形；無形，則深間不能窺，知者不能謀。因形而錯勝于眾，眾不能知。人皆知我所以勝之形，而莫知吾所以制勝之形。

故其戰勝不復，而應形於無窮。夫兵形象水，水之形避高而趨下。兵之形，避實而擊虛。水因地而制流，兵應敵而制勝。故兵無常勢，水無常形，能因敵變化而取勝者，謂之神。故五行無常勝，四時無常位，日有短長，月有死生。

軍爭篇第七

孫子曰：凡用兵之法，將受命于君，合軍聚眾，交和而舍，莫難於軍爭。軍爭之難者，以迂為直，以患為利。故迂其途，而誘之以利，後人發，先人至，此知迂直之計者也。故軍爭為利，眾爭為危。

舉軍而爭利，則不及；委軍而爭利，則輜重捐。是故卷甲而趨，日夜不處，倍道兼行，百里而爭利，則擒三將軍，勁者先，罷者後，其法十一而至；五十里而爭利，則蹶上將軍，其法半至；三十里而爭利，則三分之二至。是故軍無輜重則亡，無糧食則亡，無委積則亡。

故不知諸侯之謀者，不能豫交；不知山林、險阻、沮澤之形者，不能行軍；不用鄉導者，不能得地利。故兵以詐立，以利動，以分和為變者也。故其疾如風，其徐如林，侵掠如火，不動如山，難知如陰，動如雷震。掠鄉分眾，廓地分利。懸權而動。先知迂直之計者勝，此軍爭之法也。

軍政曰：「言不相聞，故為金鼓；視而不見，故為旌旗。」夫金鼓旌旗者，所以一民之耳目也；民既專一，則勇者不得獨進，怯者不得獨退，此用眾之法也。故夜戰多火鼓，晝戰多旌旗，所以變民之耳目也。

故三軍可奪氣，將軍可奪心。是故朝氣銳，晝氣惰，暮氣歸。故善用兵者，避其銳氣，擊其惰歸，此治氣者也。以治待亂，以靜待譁，此治心者也。以近待遠，以佚待勞，以飽待飢，此治力者也。無邀正正之旗，無擊

堂堂之陣，此治變者也。故用兵之法，高陵勿向，背邱
勿逆，佯北勿從，銳卒勿攻，餌兵勿食，歸師勿遏，圍
師遺闕，窮寇勿迫，此用兵之法也。

九變篇第八

孫子曰：凡用兵之法，將受命于君，合軍聚眾，圮地無
舍，衢地合交，絕地勿留，圍地則謀，死地則戰。塗有
所不由，軍有所不擊，城有所不攻，地有所不爭，君命
有所不受。

　故將通于九變之利者，知用兵矣；將不通于九變之
利者，雖知地形，不能得地之利矣；治兵不知九變之
術，雖知五利，不能得人之用矣。

　是故智者之慮，必雜于利害。雜于利，而務可信也；
雜于害，而患可解也。是故屈諸侯者以害，役諸侯者以
業，趨諸侯者以利。

　故用兵之法，無恃其不來，恃吾有以待也；無恃其不
攻，恃吾有所不可攻也。

　故將有五危：必死，可殺也；必生，可虜也；忿速，可
侮也；廉潔，可辱也；愛民，可煩也。

　凡此五者，將之過也。用兵之災也。覆軍殺將，必以
五危，不可不察也。

行軍篇第九

孫子曰：凡處軍、相敵，絕山依谷，視生處高，戰隆無
登，此處山之軍也。

　絕水必遠水。客絕水而來，勿迎之於水內，令半濟
而擊之，利；欲戰者，無附於水而迎客；視生處高，無
迎水流，此處水上之軍也。

絕斥澤，惟亟去無留；若交軍於斥澤之中，必依水草，而背眾樹，此處斥澤之軍也。

平陸處易，而右背高，前死後生，此處平陸之軍也。

凡此四軍之利，黃帝之所以勝四帝也。

凡軍喜高而惡下，貴陽而賤陰，養生而處實，軍無百疾，是謂必勝。邱陵隄防，必處其陽，而右背之。此兵之利，地之助也。上雨，水沫至，欲涉者，待其定也。凡地有絕澗、天井、天牢、天羅、天陷、天隙，必亟去之，勿近也。吾遠之，敵近之；吾迎之，敵背之。軍旁有險阻、蔣潢井生、葭葦、小林、蘙薈，必謹覆索之，此伏姦之所處也。

敵近而靜者，恃其險也；遠而挑戰者，欲人之進也；其所居易者，利也。眾樹動者，來也；眾草多障者，疑也；鳥起者，伏也；獸駭者，覆也；塵高而銳者，車來也；卑而廣者，徒來也；散而條達者，樵採也；少而往來者，營軍也。辭卑而益備者，進也；辭強而進驅者，退也。

輕車先出其側者，陣也；無約而請和者，謀也；奔走而陳兵者，期也；半進半退者，誘也。倚杖而立者，飢也；汲而先飲者，渴也；見利而不進者，勞也；鳥集者，虛也；夜呼者，恐也；軍擾者，將不重也；旌旗動者，亂也；吏怒者，倦也；粟馬肉食，軍無懸甀而不返其舍者，窮寇也；諄諄翕翕，徐言入入者，失眾也。

數賞者，窘也；數罰者，困也；先暴而後畏其眾者，不精之至也；來委謝者，欲休息也。兵怒而相迎，久而不合，又不相去，必謹察之。兵非益多也，惟無武進，足以併力、料敵、取人而已。夫惟無慮而易敵者，必擒於人。

卒未親附而罰之，則不服，不服則難用也。卒已親附而罰不行，則不可用也。故令之以文，齊之以武，是謂必取。令素行以教其民。則民服；令不素行以教其民；則民不服。令素信著者，與眾相得也。

地行篇第十

孫子曰：地形有通者、有挂者、有支者、有隘者、有險者、有遠者。

我可以往，彼可以來，曰通。通形者，先居高陽，利糧道，以戰則利。可以往，難以返，曰挂。挂形者，敵無備，出而不勝之，敵若有備，出而不勝，則難以返，不利。我出而不利，彼出而不利，曰支。支形者，敵雖利我，我無出也，引而去之，令敵半出而擊之，利。

隘形者，我先居之，必盈之以待敵。若敵先居之，盈而勿從，不盈而從之。險形者，我先居之，必居高陽以待敵；若敵先居之，引而去之，勿從也。遠形者，勢均，難以挑戰，戰而不利。

凡此六者，地之道也，將之至任，不可不察也。

故兵有走者、有弛者、有陷者、有崩者、有亂者、有北者。凡此六者，非天之災，將之過也。夫勢均，以一擊十，曰走。卒強吏弱，曰弛。吏強卒弱，曰陷。大吏怒而不服，遇敵懟而自戰，將不知其能，曰崩。

將弱不嚴，教道不明，吏卒無常，陳兵縱橫，曰亂。

將不能料敵，以少合眾，以弱擊強，兵無選鋒，曰北。凡此六者，敗之道也，將之至任，不可不察也。

夫地形者，兵之助也。料敵制勝，計險阨遠近，上將之道也。知此而用戰者必勝；不知此而用戰者比敗。故戰道必勝，主曰無戰，必戰可也；戰道不勝，主曰必戰，無戰可也。

故進不求名，退不避罪，唯民是保，而利合於主，國之寶也。視卒如嬰兒，故可與之赴深谿；視卒如愛子，故可與之俱死。厚而不能使，愛而不能令，亂而不能治，譬如驕子，不可用也。知吾卒之可以擊，而不知敵之不可擊，勝之半也；知敵之可擊，而不知吾卒之不可以擊，勝之半也；知敵之可擊，知吾卒之可以擊，而不

知地形之不可以戰，勝之半也。故知兵者，動而不迷，
舉而不窮。故曰：知己知彼，勝乃不殆；知天知地，勝
乃可全。

九地篇第十一

孫子曰：用兵之法，有散地，有輕地，有爭地，有交地，
有衢地，有重地，有圯地，有圍地，有死地。

　諸侯自戰其地者，為散地。入人之地而不深者，為輕
地。我得則利，彼得亦利者，為爭地。我可以往，彼可以
來者，為交地。諸侯之地三屬，先至而得天下之眾者，
為衢地。入人之地深，背城邑多者，為重地。山林、險
阻、沮澤，凡難行之道者，為圯地。所由入者隘，所從
歸者迂，彼寡可以擊吾之眾者，為圍地。疾戰則存，不
疾戰則亡者，為死地。是故散地則無戰，輕地則無止，
爭地則無攻，交地則無絕，衢地則合交，重地則掠，圯
地則行，圍地則謀，死地則戰。

　所謂古之善用兵者，能使敵人前後不相及，眾寡不
相恃，貴賤不相救，上下不相扶，卒離而不集，兵合而
不齊。合於利而動，不合於利而止。敢問："敵眾整而將
來，待之若何？"曰："先奪其所愛，則聽矣。"

　兵之情主速，乘人之不及，由不虞之道，攻其所不
戒也。凡為客之道：深入則專，主人不克。掠於饒野，
三軍足食。謹養而勿勞，併氣積力，運兵計謀，為不可
測。投之無所往，死且不北。死焉不得，士人盡力。兵
士甚陷則不懼，無所往則固，深入則拘，不得已則鬥。
是故其兵不修而戒，不求而得，不約而親，不令而信。
禁祥去疑，至死無所災。

　吾士無餘財，非惡貨也；無餘命，非惡壽也。令發之
日，士卒坐者涕沾襟，偃臥者淚交頤。投之無所往者，
諸、劌之勇也。

故善用兵者，譬如率然。率然者，常山之蛇也。擊其首則尾至，擊其尾則首至，擊其中則首尾俱至。敢問：「兵可使如率然乎？」曰：「可。」夫吳人與越人相惡也，當其同舟而濟，遇風，其相救也，如左右手。是故方馬埋輪，未足恃也。齊勇若一，政之道也。剛柔皆得，地之理也。故善用兵者，攜手若使一人，不得已也。

將軍之事：靜以幽，正以治。能愚士卒之耳目，使之無知。易其事，革其謀，使人無識。易其居，迂其途，使人不得慮。

帥與之期，如登高而去其梯。帥與之深入諸侯之地，而發其機，焚舟破釜，若驅群羊而往，驅而來，莫知所之。聚三軍之眾，投之於險，此謂將軍之事也。

九地之變，屈伸之力，人情之理，不可不察也。凡為客之道：深則專，淺則散。

夫國越境而師者，絕地也；四達者，衢地也；入深者，重地也；入淺者，輕地也；背固前隘者，圍地也；無所往者，死地也。是故散地，吾將一其志；輕地，吾將使之屬；爭地，吾將趨其後；交地，吾將謹其守；衢地，吾將固其結；重地，吾將繼其食；圮地，吾將進其塗；圍地，吾將塞其闕；死地，吾將示之以不活。

故兵之情：圍則禦，不得已則鬥，過則從。是故不知諸侯之謀者，不能預交。不知山林、險阻、沮澤之形者，不能行軍。不用鄉導，不能得地利。四五者，不知一，非霸王之兵也。夫霸王之兵，伐大國，則其眾不得聚；威加於敵，則其交不得合。是故不爭天下之交，不養天下之權，信己之私，威加於敵，故其城可拔，其國可隳。

施無法之賞，懸無政之令，犯三軍之眾，若使一人。犯之以事，勿告以言。犯之以利，勿告以害。投之亡地然後存，陷之死地然後生。夫眾陷于害，然後能為勝敗。

故為兵之事，在於順詳敵之意。并敵一向，千里殺將，此謂巧能成事者也。是故政舉之日，夷關折符，無通其使。勵於廊廟之上，以誅其事。

敵人開闔，必亟入之，先其所愛，微與之期。踐墨隨敵，以決戰事。是故始如處女，敵人開戶，後如脫兔，敵不及拒。

火攻篇第十二

孫子曰：凡火攻有五：一曰火人，二曰火積，三曰火輜，四曰火庫，五曰火隊。行火必有因，煙火必素具。發火有時，起火有日。時者，天之燥也。日者，月在箕、壁、翼、軫也。凡此四宿者，風起之日也。

凡火攻，必因五火之變而應之。火發於內，則早應之於外。火發而其兵靜者，待而勿攻。極其火力，可從而從之，不可從而止。火可發於外，無待於內，以時發之。火發上風，無攻下風。晝風久，夜風止。凡軍必知有五火之變，以數守之。故以火佐攻者明，以水佐攻者強。水可以絕，不可以奪。夫戰勝攻取，而不修其功者凶命，曰"費留"。故曰：明主慮之，良將修之。

非利不動，非得不用，非危不戰。主不可以怒而興師，將不可以慍而致戰。合於利而動，不合於利而止。怒可以復喜，慍可以復悅，亡國不可以復存，死者不可以復生。故明君慎之，良將警之。此安國全軍之道也。

用間篇第十三

孫子曰：凡興師十萬，出征千里，百姓之費，公家之奉，日費千金。內外騷動，怠於道路，不得操事者，七十萬家。相守數年，以爭一日之勝，而愛爵祿百金，不知敵之情者，不仁之至也。非人之將也，非主之佐也，非勝之主也。故明君賢將，所以動而勝人，成功出于眾者，先知也。先知者，不可取於鬼神，不可象於事，不可驗於度。必取於人，知敵之情者也。

故用間有五：有鄉間，有內間，有反間，有死間，有生間。五間俱起，莫知其道，是謂神紀，人君之寶也。

鄉間者，因其鄉人而用之。內間者，因其官人而用之。反間者，因其敵間而用之。死間者，為誑事於外，令吾間知之，而傳於敵間也。生間者，反報也。故三軍之事，莫親於間，賞莫厚於間，事莫密於間。非聖智不能用間。非仁義不能使間，非微妙不能得間之實。微哉！微哉！無所不用間也。間事未發，而先聞者，間與所告者皆死。

凡軍之所欲擊，城之所欲殺，人之所欲殺，必先知其守將、左右、謁者、門者、舍人之姓名，令吾間必索知之。必索敵人之間來間我者，因而利之，導而舍之，故反間可得而用也。因是而知之，故鄉間、內間可得而使也；因是而知之，故死間為誑事可使告敵；因是而知之，故生間可使如期。五間之事，主必知之，知之必在於反間，故反間不可不厚也。

昔殷之興也，伊摯在夏；周之興也，呂牙在殷。故惟明君賢將能以上智為間者，必成大功。此兵之要，三軍之所恃而動也。

The Art of War of Sun Tzu

Chapter I—Plans

THE Master Sun said: Military affairs are of the greatest importance to a country, for life or death, survival or destruction depends on them. Therefore they must be carefully considered. And as a foundation for this there are Five Principles that have to be studied and their nature investigated. The first is the Way, the second Heaven, the third Earth, the fourth the Commander, and the fifth the Law.* The Way is that the people should be of one mind with the ruler, for then they will live and die together and the people will fear no danger. Heaven means the Positive and Negative principles,† heat and cold, times and seasons.‡ Earth means the distance, natural difficulties, extent

---

* "The Way" or the *Dao*. Sadler translates the *Dao* as "the way." In recent times an increased familiarity of the *Dao* (or Tao) as a distinct and important concept in the Chinese thought has led to its transliteration, rather than translation. The Daoists themselves, with their specific interpretation of the *Dao,* would quote the first words of the *Daodejing (The Classic of the Dao)* and suggest that any attempt at translation would be futile, since the *Dao* itself can not be so easily defined and categorized—"The *Dao* that can be spoken of, is not the eternal *Dao*. The Name that can be named is not the eternal name." *Sun Tzu* has been categorised as being a part of the Daoist tradition, the term *Dao* typically meaning "art," "method," "principle," "path" is used extensively in other traditions of thought in classical Chinese texts, including *Sima Fa* and *Wu Zi*. No attempt has been made to change Sadler's translation of "the way," though it has been capitalised as "the Way" throughout this edition to distinguish the *Dao* whenever it appears.

† "Positive and Negative principles," is the *Yin* and *Yang* which may refer to shadow and light, or the philosophical notion of "universal balance." "Heaven" can therefore mean the climate and weather, but also the "balance" of the universe with which one must be in tune.

‡ Similarly, Mao Zedong, a keen student of Sun Tzu, found that the key to understanding war was through identifying its contradictions: "the enemy and ourselves," "losses and replacements," "concealment and exposure," "advance and retreat," and so on. To Mao, understanding the dynamic of each set of contradictions as a part of the greater totality is the key to victory. Military-strategic thinking, Mao wrote is "the study of a war situation as a whole." Mao Zedong, *Problems of Strategy in China's Revolution-*

and dangers of a position. The Commander means intelligence, reliability, kindness, courage, and strictness. Law means the formation, discipline, leading, handling, managing, and equipping of troops. These five things the leader must understand. To know them is to win and to be ignorant of them is to lose. So one must consider them to plan and investigate their conditions. And we must compare ourselves with our foe as to which Prince is the more righteous,* which general is the more able, which territory is the more advantageous, which army is the best disciplined, which soldiers are the stronger, and which side is the more just in reward and punishment. If we know these things we can determine the victor.

He who follows my plan will win and I will stay with him, but he who does not will lose and I will leave him. If he considers the advantages and takes my advice, I will put it into practice and assist him in action. But circumstances depend on advantage or the reverse, and must therefore be governed by expediency.†

War is nothing but lies.‡ So when we are capable we con-

---

ary War December 1936 p81, pp83-84, in Zhang Shuguang, *Mao's Military Romanticism. China and the Korean War 1950-1953.* (University of Kansas Press) 1995 p17.

* Translation: "...which ruler has the *Dao.*" The term "righteous" or *yi* has a very specific meaning in classical Chinese thought.

† In this passage, Sun Tzu states that a strategic advantage (*shi*) may be shaped according to varying conditions. It is only through adapting to the varying conditions, and using the favorable conditions, can a strategic advantage be achieved.

‡ "Warfare is the art (*Dao*) of deception." Ames (1993) p102. The art of deception was best displayed during the 1968 Tet Offensive in Vietnam. The full scale conventional and insurgency offensive began on the eve of Tet, the Chinese Lunar New Year holiday, one of the principal celebrations of the traditional Chinese calendar. Having agreed to a holiday truce, the North Vietnamese offensive exploded to life after the South Vietnamese and Americans had been lulled into the spirit of the truce. Before the tactical defeat of the offensive, North Vietnamese and Viet Cong forces had captured many regional cities and created havoc within Saigon—Viet Cong guerrillas attacked the US Embassy in Saigon. Ironically, this deception should not have been unexpected, if either the South Vietnamese or Americans had an eye to military history. In 1789, the most celebrated episode of the thousand year struggle for Vietnamese independence from China occurred at Tet. On the eve of the Tet holiday, Vietnamese Tây Sơn forces under Nguyễn Huệ struck the Qing forces sent on a punitive expedition from China in support of the Qing vassal in Vietnam, Emperor Lê Chiêu Thống. At the battles of Ngọc Hồi and Đống Đa, around modern day Hà Nội, Nguyễn's troops attacked the Qing forces as they were encamped for the holiday. The Qing forces were ultimately defeated and Nguyễn Huệ became the Emperor Quang Trung, unifying Vietnam and establishing its independence from China.

ceal our ability, when near to the enemy we pretend to be far, and when far we pretend to be near. Give the enemy some advantage to lure him on. Then throw him into confusion and capture him. If he is in full strength be prepared, and if he is stronger avoid him. Make him angry and confuse him. Show yourself insignificant so that he may presume on it. If he is fresh then tire him out and make divisions in his loyalties. Attack when he is not prepared and sally forth when not expected.* And those who win in the calculation at Court before fighting are those who can calculate many things, while those who do not win in this calculation before fighting are those who can only calculate a few matters. Much calculation wins and little loses. How much more does none at all. So by contemplating these things you can tell who will win or lose.

Chapter II—Operations

The Master Sun said: To make war we need a thousand four-horsed war chariots, a thousand baggage wagons, and a hundred thousand armed men. And supplies must be sent to a distance. So that with the expenses at home and abroad, the entertainment of guests, the costs of glue and lacquer, the servicing of wagons and armor, it costs a thousand pieces of gold a day to keep an army of a hundred thousand in the field. And if it is so used that victory is long in coming, the soldiers be-

---

* The entry of China into the Korean War is a classic example of Sun Tzu's maxim. With UN Forces pushing to the Yalu River on the border between North Korea and China, the Chinese People's Volunteers deployed across the Yalu, marching under the cover of night and resting during the day with the strictest light and camouflage discipline to negate US air superiority. On November 1, 1950, the Chinese struck at UN Forces and routed the vanguard of the advance. Wishing to "lure the enemy in deep" into a larger trap, in mid November, the Chinese feigned the impression of a forthcoming retreat and an inability of the lightly armed CPV to withstand UN firepower. Patrols were reduced, and US and South Korean POWs were released having been given the impression that the Chinese were planning a retreat. Accordingly, UN Forces increased their rate of advance into the Chinese trap. The Chinese attack carried out with surprise and stealth forced a long retreat—the "bug-out" of the UN Forces from near the Chinese border and back into South Korea, enabling the Chinese to capture Seoul in January 1951. Zhang (1995), pp95-119.

come discouraged and their spirit is broken, while if they have
to besiege a fortress their strength is impaired. And if the army
is campaigning for a long time the resources of the country
are insufficient. And if the soldiers are discouraged and their
spirit is broken, their strength impaired and their substance exhausted, then the neighboring lords will take advantage of their
deficiencies and attack them. And then, even though there are
some who are wise, they will not be able to do any good. And
while I have heard that a quick though clumsy campaign may
pay, I have never seen any merit in a long one. There has never
been any country that has benefited by a long war. So that he
who does not realize the disadvantage of war will not be able
to understand its advantages. And he who understands the use
of soldiers will not conscript an army twice or raise supplies a
third time. Gear should be obtained at home, but food supplies
should be taken from the enemy and thus the army will have
plenty to eat. The cause of the impoverishing of the country
by the army is distant transport, for distant transport impover-
ishes the peasants. For in the neighborhood of an army prices
are high and where commodities are dear the resources of the
peasants are used up. And when his resources are used up he
finds it difficult to till the public land. And with his strength
depleted and his substance used up, the people in the provinces
have empty houses and of the farmers' contributions seven-
tenths are consumed.*

And of the state property also chariots are broken, horses are
worn out, and of armor and helmets, bows and arrows, spears
and shields, mantlets and towers, oxen and wagons six-tenths
are lost. So that a clever general strives to feed on the enemy,
for a measure of his food is worth twenty of ours and a stone of
his fodder is worth twenty of our own. Destroying the enemy
is encouraging to our men and taking his property is advanta-

---

* Read more broadly, this chapter clearly discusses the imperative of short and decisive action. To Sun Tzu, protracted war equated to economic ruin, which in turn along
with further conscription and taxation demoralises the population and reduces popular
support for the state and government.

geous. So in a chariot fight those who first take more than ten of the enemy's chariots should be rewarded. They should change the banners on these chariots and use them with their own, and the captured soldiers should be treated well. This is what is called overcoming the enemy and increasing one's own strength.* For in war what is important is victory and not wasting time. So a general who understands war is the arbiter of the people's destiny, the master of the safety of the State.

Chapter III—The Strategy of Attack

The Master Sun said: As to the way of making war it is better to take a country intact than to destroy it by fighting. It is better to take an army intact than to destroy it in battle. Better to take a battalion, a section, or a squad of men whole than to conquer them by fighting. So that winning every battle is not the highest attainment. The highest attainment is to subdue the enemy without fighting. The best plan is to strike at his strategy, the next to strike at his communications, next to strike at his armies, and the worst of all to strike at his strongholds. Besieging a stronghold is a last resort, because it takes three months to prepare mantlets, battering rams, and other siege machines and then another three months to build up the siege-towers. The general becomes angry at not conquering it and sends his men against it like ants, so that he loses a third of them and yet the place is not taken. Such are the drawbacks of a siege. So it is that the one who handles troops well is he who causes other people's

---

* Throughout the Chinese Civil War of 1927-1937 and 1945-1949, the Red Army made a policy of welcoming defectors and Prisoners of War from the Kuomintang into its own ranks, and it was said that the KMT was the Red Army's quartermaster. Defecting or captured radio operators and the wireless equipment were especially well treated. When KMT prisoners were captured, dispirited and demoralised with their lot, Red Army propaganda teams set to work, teaching the illiterate peasants to read and write, at the same time indoctrinating them with the values, ethos of the Communist Party and its vision of a brighter future. When the Long March began in 1936, the Red Army's strength stood at around 80,000 men. At the end of the Long March, some 8,000 remained. After the Second World War (1937-1945) and the end of the civil war in 1949, the then renamed People's Liberation Army was some 4 million strong.

troops to surrender, but without fighting. He captures a stronghold, but without attacking it, and he takes other countries, but without a long campaign. He will always keep his resources intact while contending for the Empire and his soldiers' weapons will not be damaged. Thus his advantage will be complete, and this is the principle of the strategy of attack.*

In handling troops, if ten times as numerous as the enemy surround him, if five times as strong attack, and if twice as strong divide him. If numbers are equal you can fight, but if inferior give him the slip. If altogether inferior definitely avoid a fight. For if inferior numbers make a determined stand they will be captured by the greater.

The general is his country's aid. If this is complete the country is strong, but if it is deficient the country is weak. And the capacity of a prince to trouble his army lies in three things. To order it to advance from ignorance of its incapacity to advance. To order it to retreat out of ignorance of its incapacity to retreat. This is tying up the army. It is ignorance of the army that leads him to rule it like the state and to embarrass the officers. It is ignorance of the authority of the army that leads him to make its responsibilities the same as those of the civil government and engenders distrust among the officers. And when there is trouble and distrust in the army there is danger from the neighboring powers. This is what is called confusion in the army that gives victory to the enemy.

Thus there are five cases where victory may be assured. When you know when to fight and when not to fight. When you realize where the preponderance of numbers lies. When

---

* The cost of siege warfare in men and materials is the basis of Sun Tzu's strategy of avoiding this type of engagement. Better still would be to avoid indiscriminate or gratuitous use of force, instead a battery of non-violent means is preferred, such as disrupting an enemy's alliances and waging psychological campaigns. This is recognition that "war" or conflict, is not simply the domain of the battlefield, but part of a wider totality. Victory is not the annihilation of the enemy on the field, but also one's own survival. Disrupting the enemy by non-violent means is as much a part of warfare as combat. To the modern strategist, this is "asymmetric warfare," the use of "other means," such as information warfare (computer hacking, information attacks, etc), media manipulation, etc.

the wishes of high and low are the same.* When the prepared take advantage of the unprepared. When the general can act without interference from the prince. He who understands these five points knows the Way to victory.

So it has been said that he who knows his own conditions and those of the enemy has nothing to fear in a hundred fights, while he who knows his own conditions but not those of the enemy will win one time and be defeated the next, while he who knows neither his own conditions nor those of the enemy will certainly be defeated in every battle.†

Chapter IV—The Order of War‡

The Master Sun said: The expert fighters of old concerned themselves rather with not being defeated and so prepared to obtain victory. For not to be defeated lies in oneself, but the ability to win in the enemy. So the good fighter took care not to be defeated since he could not arrange with certainty to conquer the enemy.§ So they say one may know how to win but be unable to do it.

If we think we cannot win we stand on the defensive, but if we think we can we attack. The defensive is for those who have insufficient forces, the offensive for those who have a surplus. Those who are skilled in defense secrete themselves in the nine varieties of ground, while those who are good at attack act suddenly from any of the nine points of the compass. So they protect themselves and ensure victory. An apparent victory is

---

* Superiors and subordinates.

† So well known is Sun Tzu's maxim at the end of chapter 3 today, Sadler's translation is barely recognizable from the standard translation: "Therefore I say: Know the enemy and know yourself; in a hundred battles you will never be in peril." Griffith (1963), p84.

‡ Sun Tzu's title for this chapter is *Xing*, or "strategic power," or "strategic positions." This is the tangible physical power. See also Introduction on the nature of "*Shi* strategy."

§ Translation: "In ages past, those that excelled in war first made themselves invulnerable, and then waited for the enemy to be vulnerable. Being invulnerable lies within oneself, while one's vulnerability lies within the enemy. Therefore the expert in war makes himself invulnerable, but he can not make the enemy be vulnerable."

only one in the eyes of the ordinary man; it is not the highest attainment. And to win a battle so that the whole Empire says it is good is not the highest attainment. To lift the down of autumn shows no great strength, to see the sun and moon needs no clear sight and to hear the thunder no acute hearing. For what was considered a victory by the good warriors of old was one obtained easily. So the skilled fighter's victory gains him no reputation and no praise for valor. For he fights when certain of victory, and where there is no doubt he takes advantage of it and is certain of victory, for it is a victory over one already beaten, so the good fighter takes a position where he cannot be beaten and so does not let slip the moment when the enemy can be beaten.* Therefore the winning army fights when it has already obtained the victory, while the losing army fights in order to obtain victory.† So the good fighter studies the Way and holds to the method by which he can control victory and defeat.

In the rules of war there is first the size, second the amount, third the number, fourth the calculation, and fifth the victory.

For the land gives the size, the size the amount (of food), the amount the number (of men), the number the calculation (of the respective armies), and the calculation the victory. So the conquering army is like a beam compared with the mote of the losing one. And the onset of a conquering people is like the bursting of a pent-up mass of water into a valley a thousand fathoms deep.

---

* To Sun Tzu, winning a victory is based on one's own ability to be invincible, and this is where the greatest skill lies. In this tradition, the victory is due to the *enemy's* inability, not one's own ability to defeat the enemy. Accordingly, in China, there is very little tradition of the "great captains" of Western tradition of the likes of Alexander the Great, Napoleon Bonaparte, Robert E. Lee, or Erwin Rommel.

† Translation: "Therefore, the winning army fights only when the conditions for victory are certain. The defeated army only seeks victory after entering the fight."

Chapter V—Control*

The Master Sun said: Managing a large body is just like managing a few. They must be subdivided. And handling a large body of men in battle is like handling a small one. It is done by formation and banners. And the whole army can receive the enemy's attack without being beaten. It is done by the main body and reserves. In throwing in troops it is done like dropping a millstone on an egg, the solid on the void.†

In fighting you engage the foe with the main body and defeat him with the reserves. So he who handles his reserves well makes them limitless as the heaven and earth, boundless as the great rivers. When they end they begin again, successive as the sun and moon, life and death and the four seasons. There are no more than five sounds, but in the varieties of the five sounds invincibility can be heard. There are no more than five colors, but in the varieties of these invincibility can be seen, and there are but five tastes, but in their variety invincibility can be tasted.‡ In a battle there is but the main body and the reserve, but in the various uses of these there is even more limitless invincibility. Their action is interdependent and continuous like a wheel

---

* Sun Tzu's title for this chapter is *Shi* or "strategic advantage." See Introduction on "*Shi* strategy."

† In this chapter, Sadler does not fully articulate the critical aspect of Sun Tzu, that is the discussion of the use of "orthodox" and "unorthodox" (Sawyer 1993, p165) or "surprise" and "straightforward" methods as the way to attaining the strategic advantage in order to meet the enemy. Sadler appears to take a more physical interpretation of the entire chapter, entitling it as "Control," in contrast to a more conceptual interpretation of *Shi* such as "Strategic Advantage" (Ames 1993, p119). Sadler seems to anchor the entire passage in the tactical realm, rather than the strategic, where Sun Tzu really intended. Similarly, Sadler uses more conventional physical representations of "main body" and "reserves" in place of Sawyer's "orthodox" and "unorthodox." In the next paragraph, Sadler uses the terms "variety," to continue the concept of physicality or tactical dispositions, rather than conceptuality of strategic advantage. In contrast, more precise translations such as Ames and Sawyer articulate the concept as a dynamic continuum of "orthodox/unorthodox" factors, which in "combination" result in a dynamism and fluidity in and in the seeking of strategic advantage.

‡ Sun Tzu stresses the use of a variety of methods or combinations of actions or tactics to achieve the strategic advantage. This may be likened to combined strategies or joint operations; *eg* "orthodox" tactics and "unorthodox" tactics; conventional and elite troops; hard (military) and soft (economic/financial/aid) power.

that has no end.* Like the swift rush of a torrent that washes the rocks away is their impact. With the swiftness of a vulture they aim their well-timed stroke. Therefore the force of the good fighter is precipitate and his timing is sudden. His force is like a stretched cross-bow and his timing is like the pulling of the trigger. Amid the roar and thunder of the battle there is no confusion, and in all the tumult of the attack the line is intact and unbroken by the enemy. Where discipline is disorder may be simulated, where there is bravery timidity can be simulated, and where there is strength weakness can be simulated. For order and disorder depend on disposition, bravery and timidity on force, and strength and weakness on formation. So he who handles an enemy well makes such a formation that the enemy follows it.

He gives the enemy an opportunity which he is certain to take, and tempts him on by some advantage while lying in wait for him. So the good fighter relies on power and does not depend on individual persons. He chooses his men well, but he leaves the rest to impetuous force. It is this force that makes people fight.

It is like rolling a tree or rock. It is the nature of tree or rock to be motionless on a level, but to move on a slope. If it is square it stops, and if it is round it moves. So is the impetus used by a skilled fighter. It is like the force of a round rock rolling down a hill a thousand fathoms high.

---

* Translation: "The unorthodox and the orthodox mutually produce each other, like a circle that has no end. Who can exhaust them?" This concept is quite clear; that orthodox and unorthodox forces/strategies can give rise to new opportunities and situations, indicating a fluid and dynamic creation of strategic advantage. It immediately conjures to the imagination the Daoist *yin/yang* symbol of light and dark in pursuit of each other in an ever moving cycle. It is puzzling why Sadler made such a contrary translation to what is a very simple line of text.

Chapter VI—Real and False Strength[*]

The Master Sun said: The one who first decides on the battle ground and there awaits the enemy has the easier task, and the one who comes after and has to hurry will tire himself. The good fighter makes others move, but he is not made to move by them. He offers an advantage so that the enemy may be made to move as he wishes, and he checks him so that he cannot move as he does not wish. So if the enemy is resting he tires him out, if he has plenty of supplies he deprives him of them, and if he is staying quietly he makes him move. When he attacks he will do so quickly and at a place where he is not expected. And if we go where the enemy is not we can go a thousand miles without exhaustion. And to attack and be certain of taking a place we must attack where it is not defended. And to be strong in defense we must defend where there is no attack. So the best attack is such that the enemy does not know how to defend, and the best defense is such that the enemy does not know where to attack.

Very obscure and without form; very mysterious and without voice is this, but it is the arbiter of the enemy's destiny.[†] We advance and he cannot resist, for we strike where there is only emptiness. We retire and he cannot pursue, for we are too quick for him to reach us. And when we wish to fight, though the enemy may be ensconced behind high walls and deep moats, he will have to give battle because we attack a place that he must assist. And if we do not want to fight we fix on a position and defend it and the enemy cannot give battle because we deceive him as to our whereabouts. So we locate him, but he does not

---

[*] Another chapter of Sun Tzu's abstract thought. Sun Tzu refers to striking at the enemy's weakness by commanding the strategic advantage and forcing the enemy to act under one's own terms. This continues the concept in chapters 4 and 5 on gaining strategic power (*xing*) and strategic advantage (*shi*).

[†] "Form" or *xing*, that is the configuration or shape of physical power. Translation: "Very obscure, it is without form; very mysterious, it is without sound. Thus he is the master of the enemy's fate."

locate us, and we keep together while the enemy is divided. We are one united body while the enemy is divided into ten parts, so that with our ten parts we attack his one. Since we are many and the enemy few and many can easily attack few, our operations will be economical. The place where we give battle will be unknown, and being unknown the enemy will have to prepare in many places, and because he has to make preparations in many places he will have the fewer men where we attack. If he strengthens his front he weakens his rear, and if he strengthens his rear he weakens his front, while if he reinforces his right he depletes his left. As he has to prepare everywhere he is not in force anywhere. He is weak because of his preparations and we are strong because we have caused him to make them. So if we know just where and when we are going to attack we can join battle even if we are a thousand miles away. But if we do not know these things not even our own left and right or front and rear will be able to come to each other's assistance. Much less when they be tens of miles apart if distant and several miles if near each other. By arranging thus with the troops of Wu, though the men of Yue may be superior in numbers yet what reason is there that they should win? So it is said that victory is a thing we can make ourselves.*

The enemy may have more men, but they can be prevented from fighting. Plans must be made and their advantages and disadvantages carefully considered. Stir him up to see what he is doing and why. Feint to find out weak points in his position. Compare to see whether his forces are greater or less than your own. The best plan in military operations is to have no plan, so that the cleverest spies cannot find it out and the wisest people cannot fathom it.† If you plan a victory before people they are not able to understand it. Everyone knows that victory is according to some plan, but they do not know how it is made.

Strategies that have brought victory should not be repeated.

---

* These principles are the essence of guerilla warfare and insurgency warfare.
† "Plan" is better translated as "form."

They must vary according to the situation and cannot be fixed.* The operations of an army may be likened to water. Water flows on and avoids the high places while inclining to the low. So an army should avoid strength and attack weakness. Water flows according to the form of the ground, and an army gains the victory by accommodating itself to the enemy. The shape of water is never the same and military force should be infinitely adaptable. And he who thus gains the victory by adapting himself to the changes of the enemy may be called divine.† So the five elements have no permanent predominance and the four seasons no lasting position. The days shorten and lengthen and the moons wax and wane.‡

Chapter VII—Battle Tactics

The Master Sun said: The procedure in military affairs is usually thus. The general receives orders from his lord, gathers his levies, and makes up his army, takes the field, and faces the enemy. There is nothing so difficult as tactics in battle. The difficulty in fighting battles is in turning the circuitous into the straight and turning reverses into advantages. For where the road is circuitous you can entice the enemy into it with advantage, starting behind him and arriving before him. This is understanding of

---

* Strategies can not be rigid and inflexible, as they must suit specific conditions.

† The importance of adaptability in strategic advantage can be seen in the Tet Offensive of North Vietnam in 1968. It was designed to raise a general uprising in South Vietnam by the Vet Cong, in co-ordination with a push from North Vietnamese troops, to liberate the south in a decisive blow. The offensive was launched on the Chinese lunar new year, during an agreed truce. Heavy and bloody fighting followed, which ultimately led to a defeat of the Northern offensive and a crushing of the Viet Cong, from which it was never to recover. However, the impact of this bloody fighting was relayed on American TV, and significantly turned the tide of American public opinion against the war. The North Vietnamese capitalized on the changing public opinion which increasingly demanded an American withdrawal from South Vietnam. The North Vietnamese agreed to a ceasefire at the Paris Peace Accords of 1973, after which US forces were withdrawn. In 1975, the North Vietnamese resumed the fighting and without American support, the South Vietnamese government fell to the North.

‡ This chapter of *Sun Tzu* is perhaps the most telling of its Daoist tradition of thought. The allegory of water flowing and adapting to conditions, likening it to flexibility and adaptability of strategic and tactical dispositions is very much in keeping of the Daoist tradition.

how to utilize the circuitous and the straight. A maneuver like this may be advantageous, but it may also be risky.*

If you press on to obtain a decision you may arrive too late. And if you must abandon part of the army to obtain a decision you will lose the baggage train. If the troops with their rolled-tip buff-coats hurry on without rest either day or night to cover two days' march in one and go a hundred miles to obtain a decision, a whole army corps may be captured. For only the strong will go on while the weak will be left behind, so that only a tenth of the number will get through. If the distance is fifty miles then the leading general may be lost and half the men, and if it is only thirty miles then two-thirds may get through. An army may be lost for want of transport, for want of food, and for want of supplies.

He who is ignorant of the plans of the neighboring lords is not able to anticipate their combinations. He who is ignorant of hill and forest, precipice and swamp cannot lead an army, and he who does not employ guides cannot obtain any advantage from the terrain. In handling troops by deceiving the enemy we maintain our position, and where there is advantage we move. By dividing and combining we make diversions. Therefore be as swift as the wind, as calm as the forest, and as consuming as fire. Be immovable as a mountain and as inscrutable as thick clouds, but move as swiftly as lightning. Take the country and divide it among the people, allot the territory and distribute it advantageously.† Only move after weighing the circumstances, for it is the understanding of the circuitous and the direct that is the Way to victory in these battle tactics.

The military classics say that drums and bells are used because the voice cannot carry and banners because the eye can-

---

* As in the previous chapter, Sadler continues his emphasis on the tactical rather than strategic, and the tangible over the conceptual. Most importantly, Sadler translates "A maneuver like this may be advantageous, but it may also be risky." A more precise translation translates Sadler's interpretation of the "tactical" to its truer strategic meaning "Sending troops into battle can be advantageous; sending troops into battle can be a danger."

† Translation "When plundering, divide your numbers. When enlarging your territory, divide and hold your strategic positions advantageously." After Ames (1993) p130.

not reach. So bells and drums and banners are used as eyes and ears to keep the forces together. For when the forces move in unison the brave cannot advance alone or the cowardly retreat alone, and this is the Way to handle a large force. And in night fighting numbers of torches and drums are used, and in the daytime many banners, so that the eyes and ears of the enemy may be confused.

The spirit can be taken out of a whole army corps and a general can be deprived of his wits. Spirits are highest in the morning, at noon they flag, and in the evening they sink. So a skilled fighter will avoid the time when spirits are keen and attack when they are flagging or low. This is how spirit is manipulated, and it is by facing panic with control and clamor with calm that the mind is ruled. Oppose proximity to distance, freshness to weariness, and fullness to hunger, and so energy is manipulated. Not to face an ordered army with banners and not to attack a formidable force, this is to have control of varying cases. So it is a military rule not to advance against an enemy on a hill and not to resist forces descending a slope. If the enemy pretends flight do not pursue him, and do not attack one who is on the alert. Do not swallow the bait of a decoy and do not intercept a retiring force. Leave an escape for one that is surrounded, and do not press on a desperate foe. This is the Way to handle troops.

Chapter VIII—The Nine Changes

The Master Sun said: The procedure in military affairs is usually thus. The general receives orders from his lord, gathers his levies and makes up his army. Do not camp in broken ground. In cross-road ground make friendly advances.* In isolated ground do not stay. In encircling ground use stratagems. In death ground fight. There are places that mud makes unapproachable. There are armies that cannot be attacked. There

---

* Translation: At strategically vital intersections, join with allies. After Ames (1993), p135.

are fortresses that cannot be besieged. There are positions where fighting cannot take place. There are orders from the lord that cannot be received.*

Thus it is the general who is expert in the use of the Nine Changes who knows how to handle troops.† But he who is not experienced in them, though he may know the lie of the land, is not able to take advantage of it. And he who does not know the art of the Nine Changes, when he has control of troops, even though he understand the Five Advantages, will not be able to employ men properly.

When a wise man considers anything he reckons with both advantage and disadvantage. So when he reckons on advantage he exerts himself to ensure it, and when he reckons on disadvantage he is concerned to escape it. To subdue the neighboring lords you must damage them, to utilize them you must make them work, and to incite them you must offer advantages.

It is a military principle that one does not rely on the enemy not coming, but relies on being ready to face him. One does not rely on his not attacking, but on being able to prevent him attacking.

Generals are subject to five risks. That of being killed from determination to die, that of being taken prisoner from determination to live, that of being despised for being too irascible, that of being derided for being too honest, and that of being worried from too much consideration for people.

These five things are the faults of generals and are a misfortune in one who handles troops. These five risks may result in the overthrow of the army and the death of the general, and therefore cannot be disregarded.

---

* Translation: "There are orders from the ruler that must not be obeyed." Sun Tzu is referring to the nature of civil-military relations in command. Sun Tzu refers to the "situation awareness" of a commander in the field being superior to that of the ruler, and being much more aware of the fluidity of strategic advantage.

† That is, a general who is situationally aware and adaptable to every changing strategic condition.

Chapter IX—Movement of Troops

The Master Sun said: As to the position of troops and meeting the enemy. In crossing hills keep to the valleys, face the south, and keep to the high ground.* In fighting on high ground do not advance upwards. Such is the manner of handling troops on high ground.

In crossing water advance well beyond it. When the enemy is crossing water do not advance to attack him in the stream, but if you attack when he is about half over you will have the advantage. If you wish to fight do not face the enemy across water. Take up a position on high ground facing south and up stream. Such is the way of handling an army near water.

In crossing a salt marsh do so as quickly as possible and do not stay there. If you have to give battle in salt marshes be sure to make for any place where there is water and grass, and have plenty of trees behind you.† Such is the way of handling troops in a marsh.

On flat land dispositions are easy. If you have high ground behind on the right you have death before and life behind you. Such is the way of handling troops on flat ground.

It was by using these four positions to advantage that Huang-di‡ conquered the Four Emperors.

Armies generally like high ground and dislike low, they prefer the sun and shun the shade, for in fertile land and on solid ground an army is free from disease and may be sure of victory. Where there are hills and embankments you must take up a position on the sunny side, keeping them on the right and to the rear. This will be an advantage to the soldiers for the lie of the land will assist them. If you wish to cross a river wait until the water has settled down, where it has been swollen by rain up-

---

* An army positioned facing south forces the enemy to fight with the sun in their faces.

† So that the woods may cover a retreat.

‡ The mythical Yellow Emperor, considered by Chinese as the founder of the Han Chinese race.

stream. Streams in a deep valley, gorges, thick jungle, swamps, and defile must be passed by quickly and not approached. We should get the enemy to approach them while we keep at a distance, and see that we face them while he has them at his back. If your army is near precipitous places with overgrown pools, water covered with reeds, or hills covered with thick growth, they must be carefully searched, for they are places where ambushes and decoys are concealed.

If the enemy approaches, but quietly, it is because he relies on the strength of his position. If he remains at a distance and threatens you it is because he wishes you to advance. If his position is easy of approach it is for some advantage. If trees are removed it is because the enemy is likely to advance, but if he uses grass or shrubs as a cover it is to deceive you as to his movements. Birds rising show an ambush and if animals are startled it suggests hidden troops. If dust rises high in a column it denotes the approach of chariots, but if it is low and spread wide of infantry. If it spreads but in straight lines it is the work of woodcutters, but if it is scanty but moves on it is an army. If an enemy's communications are humble but he increases his preparations he means to advance, but if they are deceitful though forcible his advance means a retreat.*

If his light chariots advance his flanks will spread out in support. If he proposes peace without any oath it is to deceive. If his forces run away but stay with the chariots it is a prearranged trick, and if half advance and half retreat it is to lure us on. If

---

* We are reminded of the diplomatic negotiations between the United States and Japan from August 1941 prior to the attack on Pearl Harbor on December 7th. Planning for the attack had been in motion since early 1941. The plan had designed for Japanese negotiations to continue as late as 30 minutes prior to the attack, in order to meet international obligations and yet retain the element of surprise with a pre-emptive strike. Formal declaration of war was not to be delivered to the United States until after the attack. The attack on Pearl Harbor by Admiral Isoruku Yamamoto was almost a resounding tactical success and certainly a triumph of assessment, intelligence, planning, training, and execution according to Sun Tzu's precepts. However, the decision of Japan to declare war on the United States was a strategic blunder, which contravened Sun Tzu's most important precept of "knowing the enemy and knowing yourself." In attacking the United States and declaring war, it had awakened the American military-industrial machine bent on revenge, with which it could not compete.

troops lean on their weapons they are famished, and if they go to drink before they have drawn water they are parched. If they are in sight of advantage but do not advance it is because they are tired. Where birds collect there are no troops. If they call out at night they are afraid, and if an army is disorderly it is because the discipline is bad. Where the banners move about there is confusion, and where the officers are irritable it is because the men are tired out. When they give their grain to the horses and feed on the flesh of the cattle and break their cooking pots, an army will not return to its camp but means to fight desperately. If troops gather and mutter together quietly it is a sign that they have lost confidence.

Too many rewards are embarrassing and too many punishments cause trouble. Officers who treat their men roughly at first and afterwards become afraid of them are wanting in spirit. Those who come and make excuses want to take a rest. When troops are enraged and advance, but delay in attacking and also do not retreat, careful investigation must be made for treachery. There is no necessary advantage in numbers. Do not rush forward rashly, but if you calculate the forces of the enemy and then arrange your own strength accordingly you will win. But those who unthinkingly underrate a foe will certainly finish up as prisoners.

If soldiers are not treated kindly but only punished they will be disobedient, and if they are disobedient they will be difficult to handle. But if they are only treated kindly and not punished they cannot be handled at all. If they are ruled with kindness and ordered with strictness then victory may be said to be certain. If people are instructed in rules that are customary they will be obedient, but they will not obey those to which they are not accustomed. So if it be demonstrated that the rules are customary and reliable all will be able to cooperate harmoniously.

Chapter X—Topography*

The Master Sun said: There is land where there are roads, there is embarrassing land, there is land that helps both sides, valley land, precipitous land, and extensive land.

The first kind can be traversed by both ourselves and the enemy. If you are on high ground facing the sun and have convenient roads for provisions you can fight and win on it. Land where one can advance, but where it is difficult to retire, is called embarrassing land. If the enemy is not prepared you can advance and prevail, but if he is prepared when you advance you will not win. As it is difficult to retire you will get the worst of it. Where we advance but do not win, and the enemy advances and does not win either, we call it land that helps both. Here though the enemy offers an advantage we do not advance, but retire from him. Then if we can get him to make a half advance we can attack him with success.

As to valley land, if we find ourselves in it we must have a full force and await the enemy. If the enemy is there first, if he is in full force it is not well to follow him, but if he is not then do so. In precipitous ground, if we are there first we must certainly hold the higher position and there await the enemy. If the enemy is there first we must retreat and not follow him there. In extensive land, if it is flat it is difficult to feint at the enemy, so if one fights it will not be with success.

These are the six types of land and it is the business of a general to give them careful consideration.

So too there are six types of soldiers.† There are the active, the slack, the falling, the crumbling, the disorderly, and the runaway. We call an active soldier one who will attack ten men on level ground. We speak of slackers when the soldiers are strong and the officers weak, and when the officers are strong and the men weak they are said to fall down. When the

---

* This chapter is better translated as "Terrain," as it refers not only to the physical terrain and dispositions, but the psychological terrain such as leadership and motivation.

† "Soldiers" is better translated as "armies." After Giles (1910) p105.

subordinate commanders get irritated and do not obey, so that when they meet the enemy they start lighting independently, it is because the general does not know their capacity and it is called crumbling.

If the general is weak he is not respected, and if the way he instructs them is not clear his officers and men will be uncertain and the dispositions of the soldiers will become scattered. This is what is called disorder.

If the general cannot estimate the enemy so that he opposes many with few and puts weak against strong, his men will not confront the foe. This is called flight. These are the six things that are the road to defeat.*

The special duty of the general is to be ever watchful. Then the lie of the land may be of assistance to his men. To estimate the enemy and ensure victory, to calculate the steep and narrow places and the distances, this is the Way of the superior general. He who acquires this knowledge and uses it will certainly win, as he who is ignorant of it and cannot use it will certainly lose. And the Way to be certain of winning in war is to be sure to fight when the lord says you are not to fight, as the Way not to win is not to fight when he tells you to fight.† For when you attack it should not be to make a name, and when you retreat it should not be to avoid blame.

His country's treasure is he who only protects the people and benefits his lord. He should look on his soldiers as infants and be with them when they face a deep gorge. He should regard them as his beloved children and be their companion in death.‡ But if he is kind but does not know how to handle them, affectionate but cannot command them, and when they are disorderly cannot control them, they will be only like fretful

---

* "Road" has been translated from "*Dao*" or "the Way."

† Translation: "When the Way is certain of victory, fight even if the ruler orders you not to fight. When the Way does not indicate certain victory, do not fight even if the ruler orders you to fight."

‡ Translation: "Regard your soldiers as they were your children, and they will follow you into the deepest valleys; look on them as your own beloved sons and they will stand by you even unto death." After Giles (1910) p110.

children and no use at all. If he knows his men he can attack, but if he does not know the enemy he cannot. This is to be half-way to victory. If he knows the enemy he can attack, but if he does not know his men he cannot. This too is to be half-way to victory. Thus he can attack if he knows the enemy and his men, but if he does not know the lie of the land he will not be able to fight properly. This too is to be half-way to victory. So he who knows his men and can move without going astray is able to advance without difficulty. So it is said that if one knows the enemy and himself he can win without danger, and he who knows both earth and heaven will achieve a complete victory.*

Chapter XI—The Nine Kinds of Ground†

The Master Sun said: In handling troops you have dispersal ground, light ground, contested ground, mutual ground, cross roads ground, broken ground, encircling ground, and death ground.

Where the provincial lords light independently it is called dispersal ground. Territory into which one can enter but not penetrate very deeply is called light ground. Territory in which first one side and then the other takes it and gains the advantage is called contested ground. Where we can enter and the enemy also can enter is called mutual ground. Where the territory of three lords adjoins so that all can advance and take it, it is called cross-roads ground. Territory that when entered deeply has many fortified places behind us is called heavy ground. Land where there are forests, precipices, and swamps, so that the going is everywhere difficult, is called broken ground. Where the entry is narrow and the way back circuitous, so that a few of the enemy can attack a superior number of our men, it is called

---

* "Earth and heaven" are not physical topography, but refer to the Daoist concept of "Heaven and Earth"; the physical dimension of heaven and earth, as well as the metaphysical. "Earth and heaven" thus also refers to the nature of the universe.

† This chapter is reasonably self explanatory, and relates to tactical disposition on different physical terrain. It also deals with the use of troops and the various ways of making the most out of men.

encircling ground. Where you only survive if you light quickly and are annihilated if you do not is called death ground. Therefore in dispersal ground do not fight. In light ground it is better not to stay. In contested ground do not attack. In mutual territory do not be cut off. In cross-road ground act in cooperation. In heavy ground take it. In broken ground go ahead. In encircling ground contrive some plan. In death ground fight.

In ancient times those who were skilled in handling troops gave the enemy no opportunity to act in concert, so that the few could not rely on the many and the great could not help the small, while the upper could not assist the lower. The men were scattered and could not unite, the soldiers might assemble but could not be regulated. When they acted together for some advantage they were unsteady and when they did not they stayed still. Someone asked, "If the enemy came on in disciplined numbers how was he to be received?" The answer was that if you take a position the enemy grudges to lose you will have the initiative.

As to the qualities of a soldier, the first thing is quickness so that he can take advantage of the deficiencies of others, and through want of fear he can attack them when they are off their guard. It is just like the Way with guests.* If they can get far in, they do as they like and the host cannot get the better of them. If you take sufficient fertile land the army will have plenty of food. Thus if it is carefully nourished and without hardship its spirit will be raised and its strength increased. If you plan the movements of your troops well they will do what you did not even plan. If you throw them into a position where there is no way out they will die and will not flee. And thus dying, is there anything they cannot do? If the officers exert all their strength the men will not fear when they fall into difficulties. If there is no place to escape they will become the firmer, and the deeper they penetrate the more tenacious will they grow. And so they will of necessity light. So the soldiers will be on guard without

---

* "Guests" should be translated as "invaders."

training, and will be able to perform what is not asked of them. Without any oath they will be trusty, without orders they will be reliable. They will banish omens and lay aside doubt and so they will go on to the death.

That our officers do not preserve property is not from a dislike of possessions, and that they do not preserve their lives is not from any objection to longevity. When the order is given the officers and troops who are sitting weep into their collars and those who are prone on to their chins, but when they are sent to a place where there is no way out they are all fiercely courageous.

The skilful handling of troops is like a snake, quick and adaptable. If you strike its head it hits out with its tail, if you attack its tail it strikes with its head, while if you attack its middle it strikes with both head and tail. And if anyone asks if soldiers can be made to act thus, the answer is that they can. When the men of Wu joined the men of Yue they hated each other, but when they were put into a ship together and there was a storm they worked together like allies to save themselves. So in training horses you fix the wheel when you cannot be sure of their feet. To make valor universal is the Way to govern an army. Both strong and weak can be used according to the nature of the land. So he who handles troops skilfully handles them as one man and they have to obey.

A general must be calm and secret, fair and firm. He must keep his officers and men in ignorance of his plans and so utilize their lack of knowledge. He must change his arrangements and alter his schemes so that he can keep them from finding them out. By changing his situation and going by circuitous paths he prevents anyone from knowing what he is about.*

When the leader determines to attack he as it were makes them go up a height and takes the ladder away. When he has brought them deep into the territory of the neighboring lord

---

* Therefore preserving the secrecy of the strategy from espionage or speculation and discussion.

he puts them on their mettle. Burning their boats and breaking their kettles, they go forward like a flock of sheep, rushing on and not knowing whither they go. And when to lead the whole army into this danger is for the general to decide.

In connection with the difference of the nine kinds of land, the advantages of the circuitous and the straight and the principles of human feeling must be carefully considered. As is the Way of guests, the deeper they enter the more persistent, and the shallower the more dispersed.

When a commander leaves his country and crosses the enemy's frontier and is isolated so that the enemy may approach from four sides, that is cross-road ground. If he penetrates deeply it is heavy ground, and if not far it is light ground. If he is straitened behind and there is steep ground in front it is encircling ground. If he cannot move in any direction it is death ground. So in dispersal ground we should concentrate the mind of our force, in light ground we should keep our ranks together, in contested ground we should quickly follow the foe, in mutual ground we should be careful about defense, in cross-road ground we should consolidate our forces, in heavy ground we must assure the continuance of our food supply. In broken ground we must advance through the mud, in encircling ground we must block all ways of escape for our men, and in death ground we must show that we will not give way.

Thus the spirit of the soldiers must be to resist when surrounded, to fight when it is unavoidable, and to obey when in a critical situation. Therefore those who do not know the plans of the neighboring lords will not be able to be prepared, and those who do not know the steep and narrow places in the hills and woods will not be able to move their armies, while those who do not know how to use the country roads will not be able to take advantage of the terrain. And those who do not understand all of the nine kinds of land are not the troops for a leading power. If the troops of a great power attack a great province it is when its forces are not mobilized, and by inspiring the enemy with awe of them they hinder his cooperation. So it does not strive for alliances in the Empire and does not support any power. Confident of itself it inspires its enemy with awe so that his strongholds are taken and his province is lost.

Where you give unprecedented orders you must also give extraordinary rewards. As to crime you must deal with the whole as with one man. When anyone offends do not proclaim the fact. Make use of the offense in some way, but do not expose it to do harm. If you send men into a desperate position it is that they may survive, and if you put them into death ground it is that they may live. For it is when an army is in a critical situation that it makes a great decision.

So in handling troops you must have a clear understanding of what the enemy is going to do and if we face the enemy in an ordered line we can kill his leader even at a distance of a thousand li.* This is what is called a really well contrived operation. So on the day of the attack the barriers must he shut and the tallies destroyed so that no communication can take place. And everything must first he arranged at Court and then it must he carried out in practice.

The enemy's spies should he readily admitted and through them the points he considers vital should be learnt. We should then let them obtain false information as to when we intend to move, and this we should follow up by an immediate attack and so gain the victory. So at first we should open the enemy's door gently like a virgin, and afterwards be quick as a hare so that he cannot ward us off.

Chapter XII—Fire Attack

The Master Sun said: There are five kinds of attack by fire. The first is burning people, the second is burning stores, the third is burning baggage-wagons, the fourth is burning store houses, the fifth is burning columns. To make fires effective there must be a combination of matters. Incendiary material must be pro-

---

* A *li* is the Chinese distance usually translated as a "mile."

vided, and there is a proper season and proper occasion for starting fires. The season should be when the weather is dry and the day should be one under the constellations Sagittarius, Pegasus, Hydra, or Corvus, because under these four constellations the days are windy.

And for fire attack one must act in accordance with the differences of the five types. And when fire is started within the enemy's lines an attack from without should synchronize with it. When a fire is started the troops should stay quiet and wait, but should not attack. When they have estimated the power of the fire they should follow it up where they can, but where they cannot they should stop where they are. If they can start a fire without the enemy's lines they should not wait to do so within if the weather is favorable. Fire should be started to windward and attacks should not be made to leeward. The wind is steady in the daytime but dies down in the evening. And an army must definitely know about these five varieties of fire and calculate how to guard against them. So he who uses fire as an assistance in attacking will clearly win. And he who uses water as an assistance in attack will be strengthened. But though water will cut troops off it will not deprive them of supplies. And those who win battles by attack and do not practice these meritorious methods are unlucky and are termed wasters. So it is said that a wise lord considers these things and a good general practises them.

If there is no advantage do not mobilize, if there is no victory to be obtained do not maneuver, and if there is no danger do not fight. A lord should not raise an army on account of resentment, and a general should not fight out of anger. He should move his troops according to advantage and where there is none he should refrain. Resentment may be turned into joy and anger into gladness, but a ruined country cannot be restored, neither can the dead be brought back to life. So the wise prince will be prudent and the good general self-controlled. For this is the Way to keep the country safe and the army intact.

Chapter XIII—On the Use of Spies

The Master Sun said: If you raise an army of a hundred thousand men, and the troops march a thousand li, with the expenses of the farmer and the services of the public works it will cost a thousand pieces of gold a day. And there will be confusion both at home and abroad, while the roads will be crowded with tired men and seven hundred thousand houses will be unable to do their business. Soldiers must serve for many years, but victory is decided in a single day. So to grudge promotion and a salary of a hundred pieces of gold and thereby to remain in ignorance of the circumstances of the enemy is to be most unkind to the people. For the people will not be profited, the lord will not be assisted and victory will not be gained. So the wise prince and the good general is one who acts on this and wins, and so is of merit beyond the ordinary in that he knows the enemy's plans. And this knowledge is not obtained by praying to God* or by interpreting omens, neither does it come by calculating numbers. Knowledge of the conditions of the enemy can only be procured through men.

Now there are five kinds of spies. Related spies, inside spies, counter spies, death spies, and life spies. If these five operate together and the Way of their working is not known, it is of extraordinary effect and of the greatest value to a prince.

Related spies are those who are people of the enemy's country, while inside spies are his former officers. Counter spies are those employed in connection with the enemy's spies. Death spies are those who make false reports while abroad. Our spies are employed to know this and spread it among the enemy. Life spies are those who return and bring information. Therefore the officers of an army corps should favor spies above everything, give them greater rewards than others, and be more intimate with them. It needs a great sage to handle spies and much

---

* "God" is better translated as "ghosts and spirits." We can assume that Sadler was writing for his audience of 1944, who would have been unfamiliar with the Chinese practice of seeking guidance from ancestral spirits.

benevolence and justice to use them. For without minute care it is not possible to get the real facts from them. If the greatest care be taken spies can be used everywhere. But both those who know what the spies have not yet published and those who reveal it must be put to death.

So when you wish to attack an army or besiege a fortress or to kill a person it is first necessary to know the names of the commanders and their immediate retainers, of the gate guards and guard troops, and the spies should be ordered to be sure to get this information. And they must also find out about the spies of the enemy who come to investigate our condition, and must use them and hold them. This is where you use counter spies, and when they have found out things related and inner spies can then be used. And when these find things out the death spies can be employed to give their false information. And when this is known the life spies come back and bring their reports as arranged. And with regard to the five kinds of spies a lord must certainly know about them, and must know that everything depends on the counter spies and so must accord them the most cordial treatment.

In ancient times at the rise of the Yin house, Yi Zhi used these methods against the Xia dynasty, and at the rise of the house of Zhou, Lu Ya used them against Yin. Thus it is only the illustrious princes and wise generals who have the superior knowledge to employ spies and so obtain great successes. It is what is most needed in military affairs, for the movements of an army depend on this knowledge.

The Precepts of War
by Sima Rangju
(CHINESE TEXT)

司 馬 法

仁本第一

古者，以仁為本以義治之之為正。正不獲意則權。權出於戰，不出於中人，是故：殺人安人，殺之可也。

攻其國愛其民，攻之可也；以戰止戰，雖戰可也。

故仁見親，義見說，智見恃，勇見身，信見信。內得愛焉，所以守也；外得威焉，所以戰也。

戰道：不違時，不歷民病，所以愛吾民也。不加喪，不因凶，所以愛夫其民也；冬夏不興師，所以兼愛民也。故國雖大，好戰必亡；天下雖安，忘戰必危。

天下既平，天子大愷，春蒐秋獮；諸侯春振旅，秋治兵。所以不忘戰也。

古者：逐奔不過百步，縱綏不過三舍，是以明其禮也。

不窮不能而哀憐傷病，是以明其義也；成列而皷，是以明其信也；爭義不爭利，是以明其義也；又能舍服，是以明其勇也；知終知始，是以明其智也。六德以時合教，以為民紀之道也。自古之政也。

先王之治，順天之道；設地之宜；官民之德；而正名治物；立國辨職，以爵分祿。諸侯說懷，海外來服，獄弭而兵寢，聖德之治也。

其次, 賢王制禮樂法度, 乃作五刑, 興甲兵, 以討不義。巡狩者方, 會諸侯, 考不同。其有失命亂常, 背德逆天之時, 而危有功之君, 偏告于諸侯, 彰明有罪。乃告于皇天上帝, 日月星辰, 禱于后土四海神祇, 山川冢社, 乃造于先王。

然後冢宰徵師于諸侯曰:「某國為不道, 征之。以某年月日, 師至于某國會天子正刑。」

冢宰與百官布令於軍曰:「入罪人之地, 無暴神祇, 無行田獵, 無毀土功, 無燔牆屋, 無伐林木, 無取六畜、禾黍、器械。見其老幼, 奉歸勿傷。雖遇壯者, 不校勿敵。敵若傷之, 醫藥歸之。」

既誅有罪, 王及諸侯修正其國, 舉賢立明, 正復厥職。

王、霸之所以治諸侯者六:以土地形諸侯;以政令平諸侯;以禮信親諸侯;以材力說諸侯;以謀人維諸侯;以兵革服諸侯。

同患同利以合諸侯, 比小事大以和諸侯。

會之以發禁者九:憑弱犯寡則眚之;賊賢害民則伐之;暴內陵外則壇之;野荒民散則削之;負固不服則侵之;賊殺其親則正之;放弒其君則殘之;犯令陵政則杜之;外內亂、禽獸行, 則滅之。

天子之義第二

天子之義, 必純取灋天地, 而觀於先聖。士庶之義, 必奉於父母, 而正於君長。故雖有明君, 士不先教, 不可用也。古之教民:必立貴賤之倫經, 使不相陵;德義不相踰;材技不相掩;勇力不相犯。故力同而意和也。古者, 國容不入軍, 軍容不入國, 故德義不相踰。上貴不伐之士, 不伐之士, 上之器也。苟不伐則無求, 無求則不爭, 國中之聽, 必得其情, 軍旅之聽, 必得其宜, 故材技不相掩。從命為士上賞, 犯命為士上戮, 故勇力不相犯。既

致教其民，然後謹選而使之。事極修則百官給矣。教極
省則民興良矣。習貫成則民體俗矣。教化之至也。

　古者，逐奔不遠，縱綏不及。不遠則難誘，不及則難
陷。以禮為固，以仁為勝。既勝之後，其教可復，是以君
子貴之也。

　有虞氏戒於國中，欲民體其命也。夏后氏誓於軍中，
欲民先成其慮也。殷誓於軍門之外，欲民先意以行事
也。周將交刃而誓之，以致民志也。夏后氏正其德也，
未用兵之刃。故其兵不雜。殷義也，始用兵之刃矣。周
力也，盡用兵之刃矣。夏賞於朝，貴善也。殷戮於市，
威不善也。周賞於朝，戮於市，勸君子，懼小人也。三王
彰其德一也。

　兵不雜則不利，長兵以衛，短兵以守。太長則難犯，
太短則不及。太輕則銳，銳則易亂。太重則鈍，鈍則不
濟。戎車，夏后氏曰鉤車，先正也。殷口寅車，先疾也。
周曰元戎，先良也。旂，夏后氏玄首，人之執也。殷白，
天之義也。周黃，地之道也。章，夏后氏以日月，尚明
也。殷以虎，白戎也。周以龍，尚文也。

　師多務威則民詘，少威則民不勝。上使民不得其義，
百姓不得其敘，技用不得其利，牛馬不得其任，有司陵
之，此謂多威。多威則民詘。上不尊德而任詐慝，不尊
道而任勇力，不貴用命而貴犯命，不貴善行而貴暴行，
陵之有司，此謂少威。少威則民不勝。

　軍旅以舒為主，舒則民力足，雖交兵致刃，徒不趨，
車不馳，逐奔不踰列，是以不亂。軍旅之固，不失行列
之政，不絕人馬之力，遲速不過誡命。

　古者，國容不入軍，軍容不入國。軍容入國則民德
廢，國容入軍則民德弱。故在國言文而語溫，在朝恭以
遜，修己以待人，不召不至，不問不言，難進易退。在軍
抗而立，在行遂而果，介者不拜，兵車不式，城上不趨，
危事不齒。故禮與灋表裏也。文與武左右也。

古者，賢王明民之德，盡民之善，故無廢德，無簡民，賞無所生，罰無所試。有虞氏不賞不罰而民可用，至德也。夏賞而不罰，至教也。殷罰而不賞，至威也。周以賞罰，德衰也。賞不踰時，欲民速得為善之利也。罰不遷列，欲民速覩為不善之害也。

大捷不賞，上下皆不伐善。上苟不伐善，則不驕矣；下苟不伐善，必亡等矣。上下不伐善若此，讓之至也。大敗不誅，上下皆以不善在己。上苟以不善在己，必悔其過；下苟以不善在己，必遠其罪。上下分惡若此，讓之至也。古者戍兵三年不興，覩民之勞也。上下相報，若此，和之至也。得意則愷歌，示喜也。偃伯靈臺，荅民之勞，示休也。

定爵第三

凡戰：定爵位，著功罪，收遊士，申教詔，訊厥眾，求厥技，方慮極物，變嫌推疑，養力索巧，因心之動。

凡戰：固眾，相利，治亂，進止，服正，成恥，約法，省罰。小罪乃殺；小罪勝，大罪因。順天，阜財，懌眾，利地，右兵，是謂五慮。順天奉時，阜財因敵，懌眾勉若，利地守隘險阻，右兵弓矢禦，殳矛守，戈戟助。

凡五兵五當，長以衛短，短以救長，迭戰則久，皆戰則強。見物與侔，是謂兩之。

主固勉若，視敵而舉。將心心也，眾心心也，馬牛車兵佚飽力也。教惟豫，戰惟節。

將軍身也，卒支也，伍指拇也。凡戰，智也，鬪，勇也，陳，巧也。用其所欲，行其所能，廢其不欲不能，於敵反是。

凡戰，有天，有財，有善。時日不遷，龜勝微行，是謂有天。眾有，有因生美，是謂有財。人習陳利，極物以豫，是謂有善。人勉及任，是謂樂人。

大軍以固，多力以煩，堪物簡治，見物應卒，是謂行豫。輕車輕徒，弓矢固禦，是謂大軍。密，靜，多內力，是謂固陳。因是進退，是謂多力。上暇人教，是謂煩陳。然有以職，是謂堪物。因是辨物，是謂簡治。

稱眾，因地，因敵，令陳。攻，戰，守，進，退，止，前後序，車徒因，是為戰參。不服，不信，不和，怠，疑，厭，懾，枝柱，詘，頓，肆，崩，緩，是謂戰患。驕驕，懾懾，吟曠，虞懼，事悔，是謂毀折。大小，堅柔，參伍，眾寡，凡兩，是謂戰權。

凡戰：間遠，觀邇，因時，因財，貴信，惡疑。作兵義，作事時，使人惠。見敵，靜，見亂，暇，見危難，無忘其眾。

居國惠以信，在軍廣以武，刃上果以敏。居國和，在軍濔，刃上察。居國見好，在軍見方，刃上見信。

凡陳：行惟疏，戰惟密，兵惟雜。人教厚，靜乃治，威利章。相守義，則人勉，慮多成，則人服。時中服，厥次治。物既章，目乃明。慮既定，心乃強。

進退無疑，見敵無謀。聽誅，無誰其名，無變其旗。

凡事，善則長，因古則行，誓作章，人乃強，滅厲祥。滅厲之道：一曰義，被之以信，臨之以強，成基，一天下之形，人莫不說，是謂兼用其人；一曰權，成其溢，奪其好，我自其外，使自其內。

一曰人；二曰正；三曰辭；四曰巧；五曰火；六曰水；七曰兵，是謂七政。榮，利，恥，死，是謂四守。容色積威，不過改意，凡此道也。唯仁有親，有仁無信，反敗厥身。人人，正正，辭辭，火火。

凡戰之道，既作其氣，因發其政，假之以色，道之以辭，因懼而戒，因欲而事，蹈敵制地，以職命之，是謂戰濔。

凡人之形，由眾之求，試以名行，必善行之。若行不行，身以將之，若行而行，因使勿忘，三乃成章。人生之宜謂之濔。

　凡治亂之道：一曰仁；二曰信；三曰直；四曰一；五曰義；六曰變；七曰尊。立法：一曰受；二曰灋；三曰立；四曰疾；五曰御其服；六曰等其色；七曰百官無淫服。凡軍，使灋在己曰專，與下畏法曰法。軍無小聽，戰無小利，日成行微，曰道。

　凡戰正不行則事專，不服則法，不相信則一。若怠則動之，若疑則變之，若人不信上，則行其不復。自古之政也。

嚴 位 第 四

凡戰之道：位欲嚴；政欲栗；力欲窕；氣欲閑；心欲一。凡戰之道：等道義；立卒伍；定行列；正縱橫；察名實。立進俯；坐進跪。畏則密；危則坐。遠者視之則不畏，邇者勿視則不散。

　位下，左右下，甲坐，誓徐行之。位逮徒甲，籌以輕重，振馬譟徒甲，畏亦密之。跪坐坐伏，則膝行而寬誓之。起譟鼓而進，則以鐸止之。御枚誓糗，坐膝行而推之，執戮禁顧，譟以先之。若畏太甚，則勿戮殺，示以顏色，告之以所生，循省其職。

　凡三軍人戒分日，人禁不息，不可以分食，方其疑惑，可師可服。

　凡戰：以力久；以氣勝；以固久；以危勝。本心固，新氣勝，以甲固，以兵勝。凡車以密固，徒以坐固，甲以重固，兵以輕勝。

　人有勝心，惟敵之視；人有畏心，惟畏之視。兩心交定，兩利若一，兩為之職，惟權視之。

　凡戰：以輕行輕則危；以重行重則無功；以輕行重則敗；以重行輕則戰。故戰相為輕重。舍謹甲兵，行陣行列，戰謹進止。

凡戰：敬則慊；率則服。上煩輕，上暇重。奏鼓輕，
舒鼓重。服膚輕，服美重。

凡馬車堅，甲兵利，輕乃重。上同無獲；上專多死；
上生多疑；上死不勝。凡人：死愛，死怒，死威，死義，
死利。凡戰之道：教約人輕死；道約人死正。凡戰：若
勝若否，若天若人。凡戰：三軍之戒，無過三日；一卒之
警，無過分日；一人之禁，無過皆息。凡大善用本，其次
用末，執略守微，本末唯權，戰也。凡勝：三軍一人勝。

凡鼓：鼓旌旗，鼓車，鼓馬，鼓徒，鼓兵，鼓首，鼓
足，鼓兼齊。凡戰：既固勿重，重進勿盡，凡盡危。凡
戰：非陳之難，使人可陳難；非使可陳難，使人可用難；
非知之難，行之難。

人方有性，性州異，教成俗，俗州異，道化俗。凡眾
寡，既勝若否。兵不告利，甲不告堅，車不告固，馬不告
良，眾不自多，未獲道。凡戰：勝則與眾分善；若將復
戰，則重賞罰；若使不勝，取過在己；復戰則誓以居前，
無復先術。勝否勿反，是謂正則。凡民：以仁救；以義
戰；以智決；以勇鬥；以信專；以利勸；以功勝。故心中
仁，行中義，堪物智也，堪大勇也，堪久信也。

讓以和，人自洽。自子以不循，爭賢以為，人說其心，
效其力。

凡戰：擊其微靜，避其強靜；擊其倦勞，避其閑窕；
擊其大懼，避其小懼。自古之政也。

用眾第五

凡戰之道：用寡固，用眾治。寡利煩，眾利正。用眾進
止，用寡進退。眾以合寡，則遠裹而闕之。若分而迭
擊，寡以待眾。若眾疑之，則自用之。

　擅利，則釋旗，迎而反之。敵若眾則相聚而受裹。敵若寡，若畏，則避之開之。

　凡戰：背風；背高；右高；左險；歷沛；歷圮；兼舍環龜。

　凡戰：設而觀其作；視敵而舉；待則循而勿鼓，待眾之作；攻則屯而伺之。凡戰：眾寡以觀其變；進退以觀其固；危而觀其懼；靜而觀其怠；動而觀其疑；襲而觀其治。擊其疑；加其卒；致其屈；襲其規；因其不避；阻其圖；奪其慮；乘其懼。凡從奔，勿息。敵人或止不路，則慮之。

　凡近敵都必有進路，退，必有返慮。

　凡戰：先則弊，後則懾，息則怠，不息亦弊，息久亦反其懾。

　書親絕，是謂絕顧之慮。選良次兵，是謂益人之強。棄任節食，是謂開人之意。自古之政也。

The Precepts of War
by Sima Rangju

Chapter I—Kindness the Foundation

THE men of old made kindness the foundation of things and ruled through justice, and this is what is called orthodoxy.* When this rule of orthodoxy cannot be attained power is employed and this produces war. And this does not proceed from mediocrities. So that if by killing people security can be given to others then they must be killed.

And one who attacks a province does so because he grudges his people's lives, that is why he attacks it. Because by war, he will end war that is why he makes war.†

Thus the kind are regarded by their people with affection, the upright with rejoicing, the wise with trust, the brave with confidence, and the reliable with faith. He who is loved at home can protect his people, and he who inspires awe abroad can make war.‡

---

* Translation: "In the antiquity, benevolence (*ren*) was the foundation and using righteousness (*yi*) to govern was "uprightness" (*zheng*). Liu Zhongping, "*Sima fa jin zhu jin yi/Liu Zhongping zhu yi; Zhonghua wen hua fu xing yun dong tui xing wei yuan hui, Guo li bian yi guan Zhonghua cong shu bian shen wei yuan hui.*" (*Sima Fa with Modern Commentary*. Commentary by Liu Zhongping. Editor in Chief, Committee for the Advancement of the Revival of Chinese Culture. Editor in Chief, Committee of the Chinese Collection, National Translation Service. Revised Edition. Taipei, Taiwan Commercial Press) 1986 p.7.

Perhaps Sadler uses "orthodoxy" to indicate that this model of Confucian order was considered the "orthodox" method of good government.

† War is only used as "righteous war," a analogue to the Western concept of "just war."

‡ This represents a model of security which advocates good government through the Confucian model, that is security through harmony attained by benevolence in internal and (in the modern parlance) international relations. It recognises that civil disorder is based on quality of government, and that foreign wars are dependant on domestic support.

And the Way to make war is not to do it at the wrong season, not to expose the people to disease, and thus to show consideration for your own people. Not to wage it when the enemy is afflicted or unlucky and so to show consideration for his people also. And not to raise an army in winter or summer, and so to show consideration for both peoples.*

However great a country may be, if it loves war it will be ruined, but however secure the Empire may be, if it forgets war it will be in danger. When the Empire is at peace the Sovereign is happy, but in spring he will muster his forces and in autumn he will go hunting. And in spring the feudal lords also assemble their men and in autumn they marshal their levies. And therefore they do not forget how to wage war.

The men of old, when they pursued a fleeing foe, never went farther than a hundred paces, and when the enemy retired they did not follow more than three marches. And in this they showed their politeness.†

In not opposing the incapable and having pity on the wounded and sick they showed their kindness. In letting the enemy deploy his men before sounding their drums for the onset they showed their reliability, In striving for right and not for gain they showed their uprightness. In sparing those who surrendered they showed their bravery. In knowing how to end as well as how to begin a campaign they showed their wisdom. The teaching of these Six Virtues and their practice at suitable times were the bond that united the people. Such was the rule of the men of old.

The rule of the ancient Sovereigns was to follow the Way of

---

* Principles out of the *Sima Fa* not only show their basis in Confucian ethical and moral order, as exemplified in the concern for one's own people as well as the enemy," but they also reveal their roots in warfare of the early Zhou dynasty and early Spring and Autumn Period, before the practice of total war and the zero-sum realist "win or die" wars of the latter Warring States.

† "Politeness" is better translated as *li* or "rites." This reveals the ritual or chivalrous nature of war in this period (Sawyer 1995 p441); it also indicative of the "righteousness" of this model of security. Once the enemy has been driven out of one's territory, there is no reason for a righteous ruler, engaged in a war justified by righteousness, to pursue more than a hundred paces or follow a retreating enemy more than three days.

Heaven and establish the order of Earth.* To employ people according to their capacities and apportion the proper titles to those who administer. To apportion the proper office in establishing provinces and to bestow emolument according to rank. Then were all the feudal lords happy and prosperous and all beyond the seas came and submitted. So was strife disposed of and war at an end. This was the result of Imperial Virtue.

But after this came the Sage Rulers who laid down the regulations for ceremony and music.† They made the five penalties and instituted mailed soldiers to punish the unrighteous. By going round on hunting expeditions they scrutinized the provinces. They met the feudal lords and considered those whose ways differed, those who disobeyed orders and were in a continual state of disorder, who rebelled against what was right and did not conform to the seasons of Heaven, and who menaced the lords who were meritorious. They made proclamations to the feudal princes, clearly pointing out those who were guilty. They proclaimed the worship of Sovereign Heaven, the sun and moon and celestial bodies, and offered prayers to the Earth Empress, the spirits of the four seas, the shrines of hill and stream, and likewise revered the spirits of the former sovereigns.‡

Then the Chief Minister mustered his armies against the feudal princes, and made proclamation that whosoever walked in the way that was not correct should be subdued. Then on a certain year and month and day the army advanced on such a province, and the Son of Heaven confronted that ruler and decided the penalty.

---

* The *Sima Fa* documents the decline of civilization from the age of the mythical rulers or the "ancient sovereigns" (the "Three Sovereigns and Five Emperors") such as Tao, Shun, and Yu, founder of the Xia Dynasty) and King Wu, founder of the Zhou Dynasty. Liu (1986) p.12.

† The following passages in this chapter suggests that the subsequent "sage kings" of the early Zhou Dynasty, had lost something of the natural benevolence, virtue, and righteousness in their rule, which resulted in rebellious and unethical vassals. As such, they needed something more of a regulatory aspect to their rule, and required the occasional use of force in the pursuit and protection of righteousness.

‡ This refers to the offering to the spirits and to the ancestors prior to engaging the plans for war.

The Chief Minister associated with the hundred officials issued orders to the forces saying: "When entering the territory of an offender do no violence to the shrines of the deities. Do not hunt over the rice-fields or damage the earth-works. Do not burn houses or cut down trees. Do not seize domestic animals or grain or agricultural implements. Where you find old people or children allow them to go home unharmed, and do not antagonize even able-bodied men if they do not challenge you. And see that the enemy wounded have medical treatment."

When the guilty were punished the Sovereign and all the other feudal lords restored that province to a proper condition, providing wise officials, and raising up a good ruler, while reinstating those in lower offices.

There are six Ways by which the Supreme Sovereign rules the feudal princes: by regulating the amount of their territory, by holding them in subjection by administrative means, by gaining their friendship by politeness and trust, by negotiating with them through the power of wealth, by tying them up by cunning plans, and by holding them down by military force.

By making their hardships equal and their advantages equal you can keep feudal princes united, and by treating the small with kindness and the great with firmness you can maintain peace among them.

When in conclave with them Nine Prohibitions were published. Those who despise the weak and oppress the few must be held guilty. If rebels kill the wise and damage the people they must be cut off. If a prince is oppressive to his people at home and slights his neighbors abroad he must be retired. If he lets the land lie waste so that the people desert it he must have his territory curtailed. If he relies on his strongholds and will not submit he must be attacked. If he rebels and kills his near relations he must be corrected. If he kills his overlord and absconds he must be put to death. If he disobeys an Imperial Order and treats the government with contempt he must be beleaguered. If he is disorderly in both internal and external affairs and his conduct is like that of the birds and beasts he must be exterminated.

Chapter II—Concerning the Heavenly Sovereign

As for the Son of Heaven he must act sincerely in accordance with the Way of Heaven and Earth, and regard his sacred ancestors* with reverence. As for the officials and people it is for them to serve father and mother and act correctly toward their lord and superior. But though the lord may be wise, if the officials do not give instruction the people will be no use in war. In the instruction of the men of old the principle of superior and inferior was established and so they did not compete with each other. They did not go beyond their proper qualities, they did not conceal each other's skill and capacity and did not trespass on each other's valor. Thus their directions were the same and their intentions were in harmony.† Of old, civilian ways did not enter the army or military ways civil life. Thus they did not overstep their proper capacity.‡ As to superiors they honored the officers who were not boastful, and these officers who were not boastful were the most capable. For those who are modest are not self-seeking, and those who are not self seeking are not contentious.§ The administration of a province must gain the people's affection and the administration of the army must obtain its approval. Then their skill and capacity are not obscured. Officers who obey orders should receive commendation, while those who disobey must be put to death. Thus they will not be able to hinder each other's valor. And when they have instructed the people they will carefully choose the suitable and utilize them. And if what is taught is well practised, then the hundred

---

* Translation: "… regard the Former Sages." This refers to the sage kings of antiquity.

† This is the orthodox Confucian hierarchical structure of society, which is conducive to social harmony and by extension unity of spirit.

‡ Translation: "In antiquity, civil ways of governance did not enter the military realm; military ways did not enter the governance of the civil state. Thus virtue and righteousness did not transgress inappropriate realms." By preserving the distinction, a state would not become militarist, nor would an army become defeatist. After Liu (1986) p29.

§ This is in accordance with the Confucian virtue of humility and modesty. In fact the third line from *The Analects*, the collected teachings of Confucius states "To be unperturbed when others fail to appreciate your abilities, is that not the mark of the superior man?" Confucius, *The Analects* I.1.

officials will be efficient. And if instruction is well thought out, then the people will be happy and prosperous. And if practice is properly thorough then the people will obey instinctively.* This is the aim of education.†

The men of old did not pursue a fleeing enemy far and did not follow up a retiring foe. This was because it was difficult for him to entice if not followed, and difficult for him to overthrow them if not approached. Thus by politeness they stood on the defensive and by benevolence won the victory. And after

---

* Sima Qian's biography of Sima Rangju in the *Shiji* relates the story of his appointment to the command of the army of Qi. Defeated on the field by the armies of Qin and Yan, Tian Rangju was recommended to Duke Jing of Qi, on the basis of his skill at arms and of his skill in civil affairs, with the caveat that he was the son of a concubine of Tian Wan, who himself had been a commoner of the Chen clan and enfeoffed in the service of Duke Huan. (Sawyer 1993 p441). Thus not only was Tian Rangju descended from a commoner, he was also of relatively low status as the son of a concubine, as opposed to the son of a wife. Appointed to the command of the Qi army, Tian Rangju stated that since he was appointed above others from a lowly station, he would be afraid that he would not have the confidence of the troops and the people. Tian asked that a respected minister be appointed "inspector general" above him in order for him to carry out his duties. Zhuang Gu was appointed to this post, after which Tian made an appointment with Zhuang Gu to meet him at the gate of the camp the next day at midday before leaving immediately to take his post. Tian waited at the gate at the appointed time in vain for the aristocratic and arrogant Zhuang Gu, who on deciding that he was merely "inspector general," rather than commanding general, dallied at home to drink with relatives who had come to send him off.

After a time, Tian Rangju returned to the camp, took command, and issued his orders and disciplinary code. Zhuang Gu eventually arrived in the evening, explaining that his relatives had come to see him off and had detailed him. Tian Rangju admonished him stating that once a general accepts command, he forgets home and takes command without any other thought. He reminded Zhuang that "the enemy had already deeply penetrated the borders and that the nation was in turmoil. The Duke cannot sleep nor can he enjoy his food. What do you mean by 'being sent off'?"

Tian Rangju called the Provost Marshall (after Sawyer 1993) and asked the penalty for arriving late for the call to arms, who replied "decapitation." Terrified, Zhuang Gu sent a messenger to the Duke asking for forgiveness but before the reply was received, Tian Rangju had him executed. The officers of the Three Armies shook with fear. Later, a messenger raced into camp with a pardon for Zhuang Gu. Tian declared: "When a general has taken command, there are some orders from the ruler that cannot be accepted." Tian asked the Provost Marshall the penalty for charging into camp and the reply was "decapitation." Tian Rangju could not decapitate the envoy of the Duke, but had the envoy's aide and one of the horses decapitated and the carriage made unserviceable in order to instruct the army. After this, the army marched out. After Sima Qian, "Sima Rangju liezhuan," *Shiji*, ("Sima Rangju. Biography." *Records of the Grand Historian*) vol 64 109 – 91 BCE.

† In the Confucian tradition, education and improvement is one of the methods of self improvement that leads to harmony and order.

victory instruction has to be repeated.* This was the principle that the superior man respected.

Shun gave advice to his provinces and wished that the people would obey his orders. Yu proclaimed to his army that he wished the people to carry out their views.† Tang of Yin proclaimed to his army in the field that he wished them to have a strong resolution and so await the battle.‡ Wu of Zhou, when he was about to cross swords with the enemy, proclaimed that the people must have resolution to die. Yu had the proper qualities in that he did not use his army and so his weapons did not deteriorate. Tang did his duty in that he was the first to use an army. Wu used force in that he employed his army to the utmost.§ Yu gave rewards in his court and esteemed those who were good. Tang slew people in the city and intimidated those who were not good.¶ Wu gave rewards in the court and slew people in the city, thus encouraging the superior and intimidating the inferior man. Thus did the three rulers demonstrate their characteristic qualities.**

---

* Translation: "They used propriety as their basic strength and benevolence as the basis of their victory. After the victory, their method could be reused." Liu (1986) p25.

This is both a practical as well as philosophical point. Practically, it reduces the chance of an ambush. Philosophically, it is the practice of benevolence in rule and righteousness in the conduct of war.

† Yu, the founder of the Xia Dynasty following the reign of Shun, the last of the traditional Five Emperors of antiquity. Yu is considered one of the perfect sovereigns of antiquity.

‡ Tang overthrew the Xia Dynasty and established the Yin (Shang) Dynasty.

§ Translation: "The rulers of Xia rectified their virtue and never employed the sharpness of their weapons, so the weapons were not mixed together (to form effective tactical formations). The Shang relied on righteousness, so they were the first to use the sharpness of their weapons. The Zhou relied on force, so they fully utilized their weapons."

¶ "City" and "slew" are better translated as "marketplace" and "executed" respectively.

** This is a clear historical narrative, which describes a gradual neglect of the observance of the virtues of benevolence and righteousness. As a result, there developed an escalating use of military force and coercion to maintain political order and harmony and an increasing level of expertise in the military arts, and an increase in the use of rewards to encourage "goodness" and intimidation and capital punishment against the "bad." This is in accordance with the Confucian principle that governance by the virtues of benevolence and righteousness creates order and harmony. The lack of virtue in governance leads to increasing conflict and an escalation of responses in order to impose order and harmony.

If weapons are not of various kinds they are of little use. Long ones are used to guard and short ones to defend. If they are too long they are difficult to use in a clash. If they are too short they will not reach. If they are too light they are sharp, but if sharp they easily get out of order. If they are too heavy they are blunt, and if blunt they are not effective. As to war chariots Yu of Xia called them "Hook chariots" and they led the way properly. Tang of Yin called them "Tiger chariots" and they led the way rapidly. By Zhou they were called "Leaders" and led the way very well. As for banners, Yu of Xia had them with dark tops, so they were like his men. Tang of Yin had white ones, the color of Heaven. Zhou had them yellow, the color of Earth. And for insignia Yu had the Sun and Moon, for he liked bright things, Tang had a Tiger, for he liked mighty things, and Wu of Zhou a Dragon, because he liked its shape.

If an army is treated with too much severity the men are crushed, but if with too little they will not gain victories. If the superiors cannot find the right way of employing the people the peasants will not obtain an orderly life, and if the craftsmen do not obtain profit oxen and horses cannot be properly employed.

When those in control behave presumptuously it is what is called too much severity, and it is this excess of severity that crushes the people. When the superiors do not respect right but employ the deceitful and worthless. When they do not respect the proper Way but employ the strong and violent. When they do not respect those who are obedient but employ the insubordinate. When they do not respect those who practice virtue but employ those who do villainy. These things cause those in control to be despised and this is what is called too little severity that does not win victories.

The main thing for an army is calm elasticity. If it has this the men's strength will be sufficient. When fighting in contact with the enemy, if the infantry do not hurry and the chariots do not go too fast and get out of touch either in advance or retreat, there will be no confusion. The strength of an army lies in its not losing its formation, not losing the strength of its men and horses, and not exceeding the speed at which it is ordered to go.

Of old, civilian ways did not enter the army or military ways civil life. For military ways to enter civil life meant the deterioration of the qualities of the people, and for civilian ways to enter military life meant the weakening of the military qualities. In civil life speech is ornamental and expressions cordial. At Court people are respectful and deferential and receive others with trained deportment. They do not attend unless they are summoned and they do not speak unless they are questioned. They come forward with diffidence but retire with alacrity. But in the army they must be firm and unyielding, and when they move they must push on to the finish. Soldiers in armor do not make obeisance and those in chariots do not salute. Those in strongholds do not run hither and thither and when in peril they do not chatter. Thus etiquette and regulations are as front and rear, civil and military as left and right.*

Of old the rulers were wise so that the good qualities of the people were manifest and their virtues entirely revealed. Therefore none of their good qualities were lost and none of the people were rejected as useless. There was therefore no need of the stimulus of reward or of the deterrent effect of punishment. Shun neither rewarded nor punished, but all the people were useful. This was the best kind of government.† Yu of Xia rewarded but did not punish. This was the most instructive government.‡ Tang of Yin punished but did not reward. This was the most intimidating kind of government. The Zhou rulers both rewarded and punished, and the people's goodness

---

* This reiterates the concept earlier in the chapter that civil administrators should not aspire to be a part of military affairs, due to the differences in their arts. This is indicative of the change that was transforming the Spring and Autumn Period. In the past, the aristocracy held dual roles in administration and military affairs. As the period became increasingly contentious, professional abilities and knowledge became increasingly important.

† Translation: "This was the height of Virtue." After Sawyer (1993) p133.

‡ Translation: "This was the height of instruction." *Ibid.*

deteriorated.* If rewards are not untimely then the people will quickly wish to obtain the advantages of virtue, and if punishment is applied before they can get out of its way then they will quickly see the disadvantage of not doing good.†

There were no rewards at a great victory and neither high nor low boasted of their prowess. The high did not boast of it because they were not proud, and the low did not boast of it because they were not ambitious.‡ And where both high and low do not parade their prowess thus it shows the highest consideration for each other. And in a great defeat there were no executions, since both high and low admitted that the fault lay in themselves. The high, since they realized this, sincerely repented of their mistakes, and the low, in the same case, put away their misdeeds. So as both high and low thus shared the blame there was the greatest mutual consideration. Of old they granted three years remission after one year of service in the army. This was because of sympathy for the hardships of the people. And as high and low thus recompensed each other there was the greatest harmony. When they had attained their object of victory they showed their joy by triumphant acclamations. The chief then prostrated himself before the altar of the spirits, and acknowledged the labor of the people by proclaiming a period of rest.

Chapter III—On Definite Rank

In war ranks must be fixed, merit and demerit published, the irregular troops mustered and instructions proclaimed. Tin men must be examined and their capacities discovered, their opin-

---

* Translation: "The Zhou used rewards and punishment and Virtue declined."

† Translation: "When you punish someone, do not change his position for you want the people to quickly see the harm of doing what is not good." After Sawyer (1993) p132.

‡ Translation: "Do not reward great victories, for then neither the upper nor lower ranks will boast of their achievement. If the upper ranks cannot boast, they will not seem arrogant, while if the lower ranks cannot boast, no distinctions can be established among the men. When neither of them boasts this is the pinnacle of deference." After Sawyer (1993) p132.

ions compared and their condition decided, their dislikes remedied and their suspicions estimated, their strength nourished and their capabilities sought out. And in war too the people must be consolidated and their advantage made mutual, disorder must be controlled and those who stop made to move.*

If they follow what is correct and have a sense of shame they will keep to the rules and avoid punishment. If people are put to death for small offences these will be suppressed and much more the greater ones. Accord with Heaven, increase wealth, make the people happy, utilize the ground, and keep your weapons in order are what are known as the Five Conceptions. Accord with Heaven is to observe the seasons, increasing wealth, that is taking the enemy's, utilizing the ground, holding steep and difficult places, while keeping weapons in order means that bow and arrow will protect, lance and spear will defend you and pike and halberd will assist you.†

The Five Weapons have five uses. The long defend the short and the short assist the long. If you fight with them in turn it makes for delay, but if with all together it makes for strength. Regard the position carefully and act together. This is called mutual action.

The leader must take up a strong position, inspire others to follow him, discover where the enemy is weak, and attack there. The mind of the general must he determined, and the people must be the same. Horses, oxen, wagons, weapons, comfort, and sufficiency are an army's strength. In training consider how to be prepared, in fighting how to have something in reserve.

The general is the body, the companies are the limbs and the squads are the fingers and thumbs. War means force and fighting courage, while the ordering of battle means skill. The thing is to use what you want, to go where the going is good,

---

* The need to marshal national strength and human assets is reflective of the professionalization and the move towards total war.

† The mention of the bow (*gong*) and arrow in the *Sima Fa* dates this part of the text to a time of the Zhou Dynasty prior to the Spring and Autumn Period. By the time of Sima Rangju around 500 BCE, the crossbow (*nu*) had become the missile weapon of choice. As such it is mentioned in the *Sun Tzu*.

to avoid what you do not want and where it is not good, and to make the enemy do the opposite.

In war there is Heaven, Wealth, and Right. Not to miss the proper season, to make divination for victory and to work secretly, that is what is called Heaven. That the people should have the necessary provision and so live a prosperous life, that is what is called Wealth. That one should study to get an advantageous position for battle and to have everything prepared is what is called Right. When the men exert themselves and do their duty, that is what is called a happy company.

A great army must be consolidated, big forces must be well exercised, the most suitable control must be chosen, and the army must be ready to take advantage of its opportunities. This is what is called being prepared. When the chariots and the infantry are quick in moving and the archers make a strong defense, it may be called a great arms. When the men are calm and have great inward force it may be called a firm order of battle. When it can accordingly either advance or retreat it may be called a powerful force, and when those above have leisure to train their men it may be called a well-exercised array. When each has his function it may be called being fitted for the occasion, and when there is discrimination in this it may be called suitable control.

The arrangement of troops must be according to the extent of the ground, and they must he ordered to move according to the disposition of the enemy. To be able to attack, to fight, to stand on the defensive, to advance, retire, or halt as you wish, while keeping good order both in front and rear, is what is called good campaigning. To be insubordinate, without confidence, discordant, indolent, suspicious, bored, timid, factious, depressed, confused, self-willed, yielding, slack, such conduct is called defective campaigning. Excessive haughtiness or timidity, widespread rumors, cowardice, and continual regrets may be called breaking down of control. When the great and small, the strong and the weak, the company and the squad, the corps and the individual cooperate advantageously it may be called disciplined campaigning.

In war you must gel information about a distant enemy and observe a near one. The proper time and the enemy's resources must be considered, the trustworthy honored, and the rascals suspected. In making soldiers there is a proper principle, in doing things there is a proper season and in using people there is a proper kindness. When facing the enemy you must be calm, when facing disorder you must be quiet, and when facing difficulty and danger you must not forget your men.

At home to be reliable and kindly,* in the army to be generous and valiant, in battle determined and skilful. At home harmony,† in the army discipline, in battle observation. At home one must regard happiness, in the army the situation, in battle reliability. In drawing up an army consider disposition, in fighting concentration, in using weapons adaptation.

If men are intensively trained they will be calm and controlled and prestige and advantage will be apparent. Where principles are mutually regarded men will exert themselves, and when there is forethought and resulting success men will be obedient. When they are obedient it follows that they will be controlled, when matters are explained to them they will see clearly, and when ideas are properly defined their minds will be strong.

In advancing or retiring there must be no hesitation, and no deliberation when facing the enemy. When you hear the order attack at once. There must be no deception about names and no changing of banners.

When things are right they continue long, and when they are in accordance with the ancients they go forward. If solemn promises are definitely made then people are strengthened, and if oppression‡ is got rid of they are happy. As to the Way to get rid of oppression, one says it is justice, because thereby you ensure confidence and, through that, strength. And if the whole

---

* Translation: "Within the state, be generous and foster good faith" After Sawyer (1993) p135.

† Translation: "Within the state, there should be harmony."

‡ "Oppression" is translated as "baleful omens." Sawyer (1993) p136.

Empire is thus united on a sure foundation the people must be happy, and this may be called uniting the people and so using them. Another says it is by might by which we prevail over the enemy's pride and seize the goods he values. We attack him from without and our emissaries do the same from within.

One says it is best to use men, another direct action, another words, another cunning devices, a fifth fire, a sixth water, a seventh weapons. These may be called the seven ways of ruling people.* Luxury, profit, shame, and death, these may be called the four controllers. A gracious demeanor and increasing dignity are no more than methods by which people's characters are improved, and this too is the Way aforesaid. Only kindness† produces devotion, but kindness without reliability will lead to defeat. Let man behave as man, straightness be kept straight, orders be orders, and fire be used as fire should be.

Thus the Way of war is that when the martial spirit has been created disciplined rule must be encouraged. Then one must assume a mild expression and guide the men by instructions so that they will be disciplined by fear and wish to do their duty. So will the enemy be overcome and his territory be mastered. This is ordered by proper administration and this may be called the theory of war.

Now people's qualities have to be sought out from the masses, and this is done by testing their reputation and conduct. Those thus selected will certainly act uprightly. If they try to act thus but do not, then one must guide them oneself, and if they try and succeed, then one must not forget to employ them accordingly. It may take up to three times to be successful, for such is man's nature, and this may be called method.

As to the Way of controlling disorder, one says it is kindness, another reliability, a third straightforwardness, a fourth single-mindedness, a fifth justice, a sixth variety, a seventh responsibil-

---

* Translation: "The first is called (the use of) men; the second, uprightness; the third, diction; the fourth, skill; the fifth, fire; the sixth, water; the seven, warfare. These are the Seven Affairs of Administration."

† "Benevolence"

ity.* In establishing military administration one says receptivity is best, a second rules, a third firmness, a fourth rapidity, a fifth regulating costumes, a sixth classifying colors, and a seventh ensuring good officials so that there will be no giving way to debauchery.† In an army when the rules by which it is controlled are within the men themselves it is called responsibility, but when they are applied so that the subordinates obey them through fear it is called law.

If there is no little discussion in an army there is no little advantage in battle, for when the day arrives action will be successful, and this may be called the right Way. In battle if kindness does not do then we employ responsibility, and if there is no obedience then law, and if there is no mutual confidence then the truth. If the men are sluggish they must be stimulated, if they are suspicious this must be corrected, if they do not trust their superiors then these must improve their conduct.

Chapter IV—On Strictness in Rank

The Way of Battle is to wish to make rank strict, to make control intimidating, to make strength mobile, spirit calm and minds united. Thus the Way to make war is to select those who are of the right kind,‡ to set them over the troops, to fix the order of the columns, to form the proper columns in line and to investigate the facts and persons of the enemy. When advancing upright to bend down, when advancing sitting to crouch.§ If apprehensive of the enemy to move secretly, and if there is danger to remain sitting. If the enemy is far off you must observe him

---

* Translation: "The Way of controlling chaos are: first, benevolence; second, credibility; third, straightforwardness; fourth, unity (of purpose); fifth, righteousness; sixth, change; and seventh, centralized authority."

† Translation: "(The principles) in establishing laws are; first, benevolence; second, methods; third, its establishment; fourth, the urgency (of establishment); fifth, establishing rank (of officers); sixth distinguishing ranks with colors; seventh, officers must be dressed correctly."

‡ "Appoint those who understand the Dao and righteousness..."

§ "Standing formations should advance at a crouch, squatting formations should advance at the kneel." After Liu (1986) p97.

without fear, and if he is near and cannot be observed you must stand and not scatter.

As to position the left is below the right, and below the right is the armored section. The men stay sitting while given orders and then move off quietly. The infantry and armored men all have their ranks according to whether they are light or heavy armed. When horses are moved there is a liability to confusion and with infantry or armored men there is a possibility of panic. So they must be kept in close ranks. Kneeling and sitting, sitting and bending, they must go forward on their knees and be given their instructions at ease. They rise up shouting and the drums beat for the advance, while the gongs sound when they are to halt. They hold a stick in their mouth to keep silence, when ordered they sit to eat their rations, then they go forward again on their knees. When they seize the foe to kill him they must not look back, but with shouts of triumph push on farther. If they are very terrified they should not be put to death, and when this is shown by the appearance of their faces they shall be told that they can live and continue to do their duty.*

In an army corps when men are disciplined it must not be for more than half a day, and prohibitions must only be for a short time. It must not affect food, since if there is suspicion and doubt before the enemy he may attack and subdue us. In battle with strength you can endure, with morale you can win, with toughness you can hold on, and by taking risks you can conquer. It is resolution that holds out as it is élan that conquers, so armor is for resistance but weapons for winning.† Chariots make a close-knit defense, and foot soldiers when crouching down can resist. Armor doubles the defensive powers but weapons make for swift victory.

---

* Sadler's translation of the majority of this passage conveys the meaning in spirit, if not necessarily in words. However, the meaning in spirit is clear. This passage describes the ordering of battle formations and the manner in which they are commanded. See also Sawyer's (1986) p138 translation, after Liu's (1986) pp97-98 interpretation.

† Sadler uses the term "élan" to translate the now commonly understood concept of *qi* (or *chi*), the concept of natural internal energy that is at the core of all Chinese martial arts eg. *tai chi, qigong,* and medicine eg. *Qi* meridians (acupuncture).

Those who have a conquering spirit see only the enemy, while those who have a prudent spirit see only their own prudence. If these are mixed there is the advantage of both, for if both function together they will regard only discipline.

In war if you handle the light armed troops lightly and ineffectively it is risky, and if you handle the heavy armed slowly you will be unsuccessful. If you handle the light armed slowly you will be defeated, but if you handle the heavy armed quickly you can fight well. Fighting well therefore depends on proper combination of light and heavy. For the defensive pay attention to the heavy armed men, in maneuvering to the formations, and in fighting to ordered movements.

In battle where there is respect for orders there is an easy mind, and where there is leadership there is obedience. If the superior is worried there is contempt, but where he is deliberate there is respect for him. When the drums sound rapidly it is for quick movement and when sluggishly it is for slow. Costume that is somber is lightly esteemed, while that which is bright is respected. Horses and chariots are a strong element, and armored men an effective one for they are active and also solid. If leaders are servile they will get no service, if they are self-willed many will die. If they are anxious to live there will be much suspicion, and if they are eager to die there will be no victory. Those who die do so out of love for their superiors, out of hate for the enemy, out of pride in themselves, out of a sense of duty, and out of desire for gain. So the Way of war is to train men so that they are constrained to despise death, and if they are compelled in this way they will die as is right. The result of war may depend on the will to victory or the reverse, or on Heaven or on man. In war the instruction of an army corps should not take more than three days, the disciplining of a company not more than half a day and the reproof of one man not more than the twinkling of an eye. The greatest good is in the use of the means and the next of the end, to seize the important points and hold the lesser ones. And both the means and the end are nothing but keeping the initiative in the battle. Now the victory of an army corps is the victory of one man.

Drums are beaten in different ways, for the raising of the banners, for the advance of the chariots, of the cavalry or of the infantry, for the preparation of the weapons, for the supports to cooperate and for the advance or retreat. And when all these seven varieties are beaten the whole army moves. When the army is thus concentrated do not be slow to advance. When heavy armed troops advance do not go on too far, for that is risky. In war it is not handling an army that is difficult but getting men to handle it. It is not getting them to handle it that is difficult, but getting them to handle it properly. It is not knowing how to do it that is difficult, but being able to carry it out.

All men have their nature. This nature differs with their province. Training makes customs, and customs differ with the province. But the Way of war may change customs. As to numbers, whether they win or not is doubtful, for it is no use to boast of the advantage of weapons, the protection of armor, the strength of chariots, or the excellence of horses, nor should an army boast of its size when it has not yet acquired the Way. In war, if you win you must ascribe part of the credit to your men. And if you wish to fight again in the future you must look carefully to reward and punishment. And if you do not win ascribe the fault to yourself, and if you fight again give your men instruction and go in front yourself. Do not repeat your former strategy. Whether you win or not, do not go contrary to these principles. For this may be described as the correct way. It is through kindness that the people are assisted and through duty that they make war. By knowledge matters are decided, by bravery people fight, by confidence they are united, by profit they are stimulated and by capacity they gain the victory. So if the mind is in accord with kindness and the conduct with justice, knowledge will be a support in affairs, bravery will be a great support and confidence an enduring one.

Where there is concession and harmony people are naturally united. Where people are considerate there is no antagonism, and rivalry is only in wisdom. Thus the minds of all are happy and their powers are efficacious.

In war you strike at the immobility of weakness and avoid that of strength, you strike at the weariness of labor but avoid the calm of leisure, you strike at the greater fear but avoid the lesser. This was the administration of those of old.*

Chapter V—On the Use of Men

In war if you use a small force it must be strong, and if you employ a large one it must be disciplined. Thus the few profit by being well exercised and the many by being correctly managed. In using a large force it should be able to advance and hold its ground, in using a small one it should be able to advance and retire. If we meet a small force with a large one then we can envelop and crush it. If we divide our forces and strike with them alternately we can meet a superior force with an inferior one. And if the greater force harbors suspicion and doubt we can take advantage of the fact.

If the enemy gets an advantage in position and tries to exploit it we must leave our banners and retire and then lure him on so that we can counter-attack. If he has superior numbers we must reconnoiter and estimate his strength and then meet his enveloping movement. If his numbers are inferior, or if he is timid, we should avoid him and draw out his lines.

In war one should have the wind behind, high ground behind and on the right, and steep precipitous ground on the left. Wet places and difficult broken country must be passed by, and round tortoise-backed slopes are to be avoided.

---

* This chapter is a reasonably self explanatory chapter on practical administration and training. There remains a strong emphasis on the moral virtues of benevolence and righteousness, particularly in terms of administration and motivation of troops respectively. Sadler's translation does contain some less than precise translations in this chapter, although the meaning is generally well conveyed. Any incongruities of translation in this chapter have been re-translated in the notes where they are critical to the conceptualisation of moral virtue. Where they have no real effect on the meaning of the passage, they have been left unremarked.

In war we have to fit out an army and then observe how it works, and to watch the enemy before moving. If the enemy waits for you to move, stand on the defensive and do not sound your drums for the onset. Wait and see how he will use his forces, and if he attacks mass your men and reconnoiter. In deciding whether to use small or large forces you must watch how the situation changes, and in ordering the advance or retreat you must calculate the strength of the enemy's defense. In a risky situation you must estimate the extent of his fear, when things are quiet you must observe if he is sluggish, when he is on the move if he is irresolute, and when he attacks if he is disciplined. We attack him when irresolute, throw in reinforcements where he wavers, reach the climax when he gives way, and overthrow the order of his ranks. When he cannot escape we upset his schemes, deprive him of his plans, and take advantage of his panic. Do not stop the pursuit when he flees, but should he stop on the road then be wary and consider.

When you approach the enemy capital there must be a clear road to advance, and when you retire you must have a plan for retreat.

In war, if you move before the enemy you may be routed, and if after him you may become afraid of him. If you rest you may become sluggish and if you do not you may be routed. If you rest a long time it will moreover make you timid.

"Stopping affectionate letters" is a phrase that signifies banishing all thoughts of home-sickness. "Choosing good men and then arming them" is another that means increasing the strength of the forces. "Casting away encumbrances and limiting food" means giving free play to the resolution. These are maxims of the men of old.

Wu Zi on the Art of War
(CHINESE TEXT)
吳　子　直　解

吳起儒服以兵機見魏文侯。文侯曰：寡人不好軍旅之事。起曰：臣以見占隱，以往察來，主君何言與心違？今君四時使斬離皮革，掩以朱漆，畫以丹青，爍以犀象。冬日衣之則不溫，夏日衣之則不涼。為長戟二丈四尺，短戟一丈二尺。革車掩戶，縵輪籠轂，觀之於目則不麗，乘之於田則不輕，不識主君安用此也？若以備進戰退守，而不求能用者，譬猶伏雞之搏狸，乳犬之犯虎，雖有鬪心，隨之死矣。昔承桑氏之君，修德廢武，以滅其國家。有扈氏之君，恃衆好勇，以喪其社稷。明主鑒茲，必內修文德，外治武備。故當敵而不進，無逮於義矣；僵屍而哀之，無逮於仁矣。於是文侯身自布席，夫人捧觴，醮吳起於廟，立為大將，守西河。與諸侯大戰七十六，全勝六十四，餘則均解。闢土四面，拓地千里，皆起之功也。

圖國第一
第一章

吳子曰：昔之圖國家者，必先教百姓而親萬民。有四不和：不和於國，不可以出軍；不和於軍，不可以出陣；不和於陣，不可以進戰；不和於戰，不可以決勝。是以有道之主，將用其民，先和而後造大事。不敢信其私謀，必告於祖廟，啟於元龜，參之天時，吉乃後舉。民知君之愛其命，惜其死，若此之至，而與之臨難，則士以進死為榮，退生為辱矣。

第二章

吳子曰：夫道者，所以反本復始。義者，所以行事立功。謀者，所以違害就利。要者，所以保業守成。若行不合道，舉不合義，而處大居貴，患必及之。是以聖人綏之以道，理之以義，動之以禮，撫之以仁。此四德者，修之則興，廢之則衰。故成湯討桀而夏民喜說，周武伐紂而殷人不非。與順天人，故能然矣。

第三章

吳子曰：凡制國治軍，必教之以禮，勵之以義，使有恥也。夫人有恥，在大足以戰，在小足以守矣。然戰勝易，守勝難。故曰：天下戰國，五勝者禍，四勝者弊，三勝者霸，二勝者王，一勝者帝。是以數勝得天下者稀，以亡者眾。

第四章

吳子曰：凡兵之所起者有五：一曰爭名，二曰爭利，三曰積惡，四曰內亂，五曰因饑。其名又有五：一曰義兵，二曰強兵，三曰剛兵，四曰暴兵，五曰逆兵。禁暴救亂曰義，恃眾以伐曰強，因怒興師曰剛，棄禮貪利曰暴，國亂人疲舉事動眾曰逆。五者之服，各有其道，義必以禮服，強必以謙服，剛必以辭服，暴必以詐服，逆必以權服。

第 五 章

武侯問曰：願聞治兵、料人、固國之道。起對曰：古之明
王，必謹君臣之禮，飾上下之儀，安集吏民，順俗而教，
簡募良材，以備不虞。昔齊桓募士五萬，以霸諸侯。晉
文召為前行四萬，以獲其志。秦穆置陷陳三萬，以服鄰
敵。故強國之君，必料其民。民有膽勇氣力者，聚為一
卒。樂以進戰效力、以顯其忠勇者，聚為一卒。能踰高
超遠、輕足善走者，聚為一卒。王臣失位而欲見功於上
者，聚為一卒。棄城去守、欲除其醜者，聚為一卒。此五
者，軍之練銳也。有此三千人，內出可以決圍，外入可以
屠城矣。

第 六 章

武侯問曰：願聞陳必定、守必固、戰必勝之道。起對曰：
立見且可，豈直聞乎！君能使賢者居上，不肖者處下，則
陳已定矣。民安其田宅，親其有司，則守已固矣。百姓皆
是吾君而非鄰國，則戰已勝矣。武侯嘗謀事，羣臣莫能
及，罷朝而有喜色。起進曰：昔楚莊王嘗謀事，羣臣莫
能及，罷朝而有憂色。申公問曰：君有憂色，何也？曰：
寡人聞之，世不絕聖，國不乏賢，能得其師者王，能得其
友者霸。今寡人不才，而羣臣莫及者，楚國其殆矣。此楚
莊王之所憂，而君說之，臣竊懼矣。於是武侯有慚色。

料 敵 第 二

第 一 章

武侯謂吳起曰：今秦脅吾西，楚帶吾南，趙衝吾北，齊
臨吾東，燕絕吾後，韓據吾前。六國之兵四守，勢甚不
便，憂此奈何？起對曰：夫安國家之道，先戒為寶。今

君已戒,禍其遠矣。臣請論六國之俗:夫齊陳重而不堅,秦陳散而自鬥,楚陳整而不久,燕陳守而不走,三晉陳治而不用。夫齊性剛,其國富,君臣驕奢而簡於細民,其政寬而祿不均,一陳兩心,前重後輕,故重而不堅。擊此之道,必三分之,獵其左右,脅而從之,其陳可壞。秦性強,其地險,其政嚴,其賞罰信,其人不讓,皆有鬥心,故散而自戰。擊此之道,必先示之以利而引去之,士貪於得而離其將,乘乖獵散,設伏投機,其將可取。楚性弱,其地廣,其政騷,其民疲,故整而不久。擊此之道,襲亂其屯,先奪其氣。輕進速退,弊而勞之,勿與爭戰,其軍可敗。燕性慤,其民慎,好勇義,寡詐謀,故守而不走。擊此之道,觸而迫之,陵而遠之,馳後之,則上疑而下懼,謹我車騎必避之路,其將可虜。三晉者,中國也,其性和,其政平,其民疲於戰,習於兵,輕其將,薄其祿,士無死志,故治而不用。擊此之道,阻陳而壓之,眾來則拒之,去則追之,以倦其師。此其勢也。然則一軍之中,必有虎賁之士;力輕扛鼎,足輕戎馬,搴旗斬將,必有能者。若此之等,選而別之,愛而貴之,是謂軍命。其有工用五兵、材力健疾、志在吞敵者,必加其爵列,可以決勝。厚其父母妻子,勸賞畏罰,此堅陳之士,可與持久。能審料此,可以擊倍。武侯曰:善。

第二章

吳子曰:凡料敵有不卜而與之戰者八:一曰疾風大寒,早興寤遷,剖冰濟水,不憚艱難;二曰盛夏炎熱,晏興無間,行驅饑渴,務於取遠;三曰師既淹久,糧食無有,百姓怨怒,妖祥數起,上不能止;四曰軍資既竭;五曰徒眾不多,水地不利,人馬疾疫,四鄰不至;六曰道遠日暮,士眾勞懼,倦而夫食,解甲而息;七曰將薄吏輕,士卒不固，三軍數驚，師徒無助；八曰陳而未定，舍而未畢，行阪涉險，半隱半出。諸如此者，擊之勿疑。有不占而避之者六：一曰土地廣大，人民富眾；二曰上愛其下，惠施流布；三曰賞信刑察，發必得時；四曰陳功居列，任賢使能；五曰師徒之眾，兵甲之精；六曰四鄰之助，大國之援。凡此不如敵人，避之勿疑。所謂見可而進，知難而退也。

第 三 章

武侯問曰：　吾欲觀敵之外以知其內，察其進以知其止，以定勝負，可得聞乎？起對曰：敵人之來，蕩蕩無慮，旌旗煩亂，人馬數顧，一可擊十，必使無措。諸侯未會，君臣未和，溝壘未成，禁令未施，三軍洶洶，欲前不能，欲去不敢，以半擊倍，百戰不殆。"

第 四 章

武侯問敵必可擊之道。起對曰：用兵必須審敵虛實而趨其危。敵人遠來新至、行列未定可擊，既食未設備可擊，奔走可擊，勤勞可擊，未得地利可擊，失時不從可擊，涉長道後行未息可擊，涉水半渡可擊，險道狹路可擊，旌旗亂動可擊，陳數移動可擊，將離士卒可擊，心怖可擊。凡若此者，選銳衝之，分兵繼之，急擊勿疑。

治 兵 第 三
第 一 章

武侯問曰：用兵之道何先？起對曰：先明四輕、二重、一信。曰：何謂也？對曰：使地輕馬，馬輕車，車輕人，人輕戰。明知險易，則地輕馬。芻秣以時，則馬輕車。膏鐧有餘，則車輕人。鋒銳甲堅，則人輕戰。進有重賞，退有重刑。行之以信。審能達此，勝之主也。

第二章

武侯問曰：兵何以為勝？起對曰：以治為勝。又問曰：不在眾乎？起對曰：若法令不明，賞罰不信，金之不止，鼓之不進，雖有百萬，何益於用。所謂治者，居則有禮，動則有威，進不可當，退不可追，前卻有節，左右應麾，雖絕成陳，雖散成行。與之安，與之危，其眾可合而不可離，可用而不可疲，投之所往，天下莫當，名曰父子之兵。

第三章

吳子曰：凡行軍之道，無犯進止之節，無失飲食之適，無絕人馬之力。此三者，所以任其上令。任其上令，則治之所由生也。若進止不度，飲食不適，馬疲人倦而不解舍，所以不任其上令。上令既廢，以居則亂，以戰則敗。

第四章

吳子曰：凡兵戰之場，止屍之地。必死則生，幸生則死。其善將者，如坐漏船之中，伏燒屋之下，使智者不及謀，勇者不及怒，受敵可也。故曰：用兵之害，猶豫最大；三軍之災，生於狐疑。

第五章

吳子曰：夫人常死其所不能，敗其所不便。故用兵之法，教戒為先。一人學戰，教成十人。十人學戰，教成百人。百人學戰，教成千人。千人學戰，教成萬人。萬人學戰，教成三軍。以近待遠，以佚待勞，以飽待饑。圓而方之，坐而起之，行而止之，左而右之，前而後之，分而合之，結而解之。每變皆習，乃授其兵。是謂將事。

第六章

吳子曰：教戰之令，短者持矛戟，長者持弓弩，強者持旌旗，勇者持金鼓，弱者給廝養，智者為謀主。鄉里相比，什伍相保。一鼓整兵，二鼓習陳，三鼓趨食，四鼓嚴辨，五鼓就行。聞鼓聲合，然後舉旗。

第七章

武侯問曰：三軍進止。豈有道乎？起對曰：無當天竈，無當龍頭。天竈者，大谷之口。龍頭者，大山之端。必左青龍，右白虎，前朱雀，後玄武，招搖在上，從事於下。將戰之時，審候風所從來。風順致呼而從之，風逆堅陳以待之。

第八章

武侯問曰：凡畜卒騎，豈有方乎？起對曰：夫馬必安其處所，適其水草，節其饑飽。冬則溫廄，夏則涼廡。刻剔毛鬣，謹落四下。戢其耳目，無令驚駭。習其馳逐，閑其進止。人馬相親，然後可使。車騎之具，鞍、勒、銜、轡，必令完堅。凡馬不傷於末，必傷於始；不傷於饑，必傷於飽。日暮道遠，必數上下。寧勞於人，慎勿勞馬。常令有餘，備敵覆我。能明此者，橫行天下。

論將第四

第一章

吳子曰：夫總文武者，軍之將也。兼剛柔者，兵之事也。凡人論將，常觀於勇。勇之於將，乃數分之一耳。夫勇者必輕合，輕合而不知利，未可也。故將之所慎者五：一曰理，二曰備，三曰果，四曰戒，五曰約。理者，治眾如治寡。備者，出門如見敵。果者，臨敵不懷生。戒者，雖克如始戰。約者，法令省而不煩。受命而不辭家，敵破而後言返，將之禮也。故師出之日，有死之榮，無生之辱。

第二章

吳子曰：凡兵有四機：一曰氣機，二曰地機，三曰事機，四曰力機。三軍之眾，百萬之師，張設輕重，在於一人，是謂氣機。路狹道險，名山大塞，十夫所守，千夫不過，是謂地機。善行間諜，輕兵往來，分散其眾，使其君臣相怨，上下相咎，是謂事機。車堅管轄，舟利櫓楫，士習戰陳，馬閑馳逐，是謂力機。知此四者，乃可為將。然其威、德、仁、勇，必足以率下安眾，怖敵決疑。施令而下不敢犯，所在而寇不敢敵。得之國強，去之國亡。是謂良將。

第三章

吳子曰：夫鼙鼓金鐸，所以威耳。旌旗麾幟，所以威目。禁令刑罰，所以威心。耳威於聲，不可不清。目威於色，不可不明。心威於刑，不可不嚴。三者不立，雖有其國，必敗於敵。故曰：將之所麾，莫不從移；將之所指，莫不前死。

第四章

吳子曰：凡戰之要，必先占其將而察其才。因其形而用權，則不勞而功舉。其將愚而信人，可詐而誘；貪而忽名，可貨而賂；輕變無謀，可勞而困。上富而驕，下貧而怨，可離而間。進退多疑，其眾無依，可震而走。士輕其將而有歸志，塞易開險，可邀而取。進道易，退道難，可來而前。進道險，退道易，可薄而擊。居軍下濕，水無所通，霖雨數至，可灌而沉。居軍荒澤，草楚幽穢，風飆數至，可楚而滅。停久不移，將士懈怠，其軍不備，可潛而襲。

第五章

武侯問曰：兩軍相望，不知其將，我欲相之，其術如何？起對曰：令賤而勇者，將輕銳以嘗之。務於北，無務於得，觀敵之來，一坐一起，其政以理，其追北佯為不及，其見利佯為不知，如此將者，名為智將，勿與戰也。若其眾讙譁，旌旗煩亂，其卒自行自止，其兵或縱或橫，其追北恐不及，見利恐不得，此為愚將，雖眾可獲。

應變第五
第一章

武侯問曰：車堅馬良，將勇兵強，卒遇敵人，亂而失行，則如之？吳起對曰：凡戰之法，晝以旌旗旛麾為節，夜以金鼓笳笛為節。麾左而左，麾右而右。鼓之則進，金之則止。一吹而行，再吹而聚，不從令者誅。三軍服威，士卒用命，則戰無強敵，攻無堅陳矣。

第二章

武侯問曰：若敵眾我寡，為之奈何？起對曰：避之於易，邀之於阨。故曰：以一擊十，莫善於阨；以十擊百，莫善於險；以千擊萬，莫善於阻。今有少卒卒起，擊金鳴鼓於阨路，雖有大眾，莫不驚動。故曰：用眾者務易，用少者務隘。

第三章

武侯問曰：有師甚眾，既武且勇；背大阻險，右山左水；深溝高壘，守以強弩；退如山移，進如風雨，糧食又多。難與長守。則如之何？起對曰：大哉問乎！此非車騎之力，聖人之謀也。能備千乘萬騎，兼之徒步，分為五軍，各軍一衢。夫五軍五衢，敵人必惑，莫知所加。敵若堅守以固其兵，急行間諜以觀其慮。彼聽吾說，解之而去。不聽吾說，斬使焚書，分為五戰。戰勝勿追，不勝疾走。如是佯北，安行疾鬪，一結其前，一絕其後。兩軍銜枚，或左或右，而襲其處。五軍交至，必有其利。此擊強之道也。

第四章

武侯問曰：敵近而薄我，欲去無路，我眾甚懼，為之奈何？起對曰：為此之術，若我眾彼寡，分而乘之。彼眾我寡，以方從之。從之無息，雖眾可服。"

第五章

武侯問曰：若遇敵於谿谷之間，傍多險阻，彼眾我寡，為之奈何？起對曰：遇諸丘陵、林谷、深山、大澤，疾行亟去，勿得從容。若高山深谷，卒然相遇，必先鼓譟而乘之。進弓與弩，且射且虜。審察其治，亂則擊之勿疑。

第六章

武侯問曰：左右高山，地甚狹迫，卒遇敵人，擊之不敢，去之不得，為之奈何？起對曰：此謂谷戰，雖衆不用。募吾材士與敵相當，輕足利兵以為前行，分車列騎隱於四旁，相去數里，無見其兵，敵必堅陳，進退不敢。於是出旌列旆，行出山外營之，敵令得休。此谷戰之法也。

第七章

武侯問曰：吾與敵相遇大水之澤，傾輪沒轅，水薄車騎，舟楫不設，進退不得，為之奈何？起對曰：此謂水戰，無用車騎，且留其傍。登高四望，必得水情。知其廣狹，盡其淺深，乃可為奇以勝之。敵若絕水，半渡而薄之。

第八章

武侯問曰：天久連雨，馬陷車止，四面受敵，三軍驚駭，為之奈何？起對曰：凡用車者，陰濕則停，陽燥則起；貴高賤下，馳其強車；若進若止，必從其道。敵人若起，必逐其迹。

第九章

武侯問曰：暴寇卒來，掠吾田野，取吾牛馬，則如之何？起對曰：暴寇之來，必慮其強，善守勿應。彼將暮去，其裝必重，其心必恐，還退務速，必有不屬。追而擊之，其兵可覆。

第十章

吳子曰：凡攻敵圍城之道，城邑既破，各入其宮。御其祿秩，收其器物。軍之所至，無刊其木、發其屋、取其粟、殺其六畜、燔其積聚，示民無殘心。其有請降，許而安之。

勵士第六

第一章

武侯問曰：嚴刑明賞，足以勝乎？起對曰：嚴明之事，臣不能悉。雖然，非所恃也。夫發號施令而人樂聞，興師動眾而人樂戰，交兵接刃而人樂死。此三者，人主之所恃也。武侯曰：致之奈何？對曰：君舉有功而進饗之，無功而勵之。於是武侯設坐廟庭為三行饗士大夫。上功坐前行，餚席兼重器、上牢。次功坐中行，餚席器差減。無功坐後行，餚席無重器。饗畢而出，又頒賜有功者父母妻子於廟門外，亦以功為差。有死事之家，歲遣使者勞賜其父母，著不忘於心。行之三年，秦人興師，臨於西河，魏士聞之，不待吏令，介冑而奮擊之者以萬數。武侯召吳起而謂曰：子前日之教行矣。起對曰：臣聞人有短長，氣有盛衰。君試發無功者五萬人，臣請率以當之。脫其不勝，取笑於諸侯，失權於天下矣。今使一死賊伏於曠野，千人追之，莫不梟視狼顧。何者？恐其暴起而害己也。是以一人投命，足懼千夫。今臣以五萬之眾，而為一死賊，率以討之，固難敵矣。於是武侯從之，兼車五百乘，騎三千匹，而破秦五十萬眾，此勵士之功也。先戰一日，吳起令三軍曰：諸吏士當從受敵。車騎與徒，若車不得車，騎不得騎，徒不得徒，雖破軍皆無功。故戰之日，其令不煩而威震天下。

Wu Zi on the Art of War

Introduction

WU QI,* wearing the costume of a scholar, showed military plans to Marquis Wen of Wei. The Marquis Wen said: "I do not like military affairs." Wu Qi said: "A minister demonstrates secret divinations and from the present deduces the future, so why does the lord disagree with him? In the four seasons the lord uses skins and leather for clothes, scarlet and lacquer for ornaments, red and blue for paintings and ivory for display. In winter they do not warm him and in summer they do not cool him. If he makes twenty-four foot long spears and twelve foot short ones and many war chariots with their leather covered wheels, they may not be beautiful to look at nor easy to ride in over the fields, but with these things he can make offensive or defensive war. Still if he does not find out one who can use these things properly it is like a hen facing a badger or a puppy attacking a tiger. They may have a fighting spirit, but if they persist they will die.

"In ancient times there was Lord Cheng Sang who practised righteousness and abolished militarism and thereby brought his country to ruin, and there was also Lord Yu Hu who relied on his forces and loved valor and brought sorrow to his ancestral deities.† The wise ruler meditates on these things and cultivates righteousness within his country, but prepares for military operations outside it. If he does not advance against the enemy

---

* Named Wu Qi, known also as Wu Zi (Master Wu).

† The ancestral spirits would be in sorrow if the ancestral rites could not be performed, either through neglect by the extermination of the clan; or the loss of the ancestral temples by conquest or destruction.

when he comes it is not righteousness, and if he is sorry that men are killed it is not benevolence."*

On hearing this the Marquis Wen himself placed the mat and his wife offered the wine-cup, and they brought Wu Qi to the ancestral shrine and made him general. He guarded the four rivers and fought seventy-six great battles with the neighboring lords, attaining complete victory in sixty-four, while the rest were drawn. On all sides he reclaimed country and extended the cultivated land for a thousand li.† All this was owing to the ability of Wu Qi.

Section I—The Government of a Country
Chapter I

The Master Wu said: "In ancient times he who governed a country always first instructed the peasants and treated the population kindly. There are four matters in which concord may be lacking. Want of concord‡ in the country so that the army cannot be mobilized. Want of it in the army so that it cannot take the field. Want of it in the camp so that it cannot take the offensive. And want of it in the battle so that it cannot win. Therefore the leader who has method so handles the people that there is concord and thus does great things. He does not put his trust in his own plans alone, but lays them before the ancestral shrine, and enquires also by tortoise divination to see if all is according to heaven's season, and if the omens are good then he makes war.§ If the people know that the prince grudges

---

* Wu Qi sets the theme of his treatise in the first chapter: that is that domestic security is founded on Confucian virtues, such as humaneness, benevolence, and righteousness, which bring social harmony and order. External security is dependant on the same Confucian principles through the virtuous behaviour which embraces benevolence, and only engaging in the use of force and arms with righteous cause.

† *Li* is the Chinese mile

‡ "Harmony" is the better translation. Social harmony is the foundation of national unity at time of war, and it must be cultivated by benevolent rule.

§ The combination of offering the plans to the ancestral spirits and seeking guidance by divination ensures that the planning is both sanctioned and ritually correct in form. Tortoise shells used for divination, or "oracle bones," carry the oldest recorded Chinese script dating from the Shang Dynasty. Questions to be divined were written on the tor-

their lives and regrets their deaths, and will not fail to face difficulties with them, then the officers will think it a glorious thing to advance and die and shameful to retreat and live."

Chapter II

The Master Wu said: "What is called method* is returning to the beginning to obtain the fundamental things. What is called right is acquiring efficiency by the practice of things. What is called planning is avoiding damage and gaining advantage. And what is essential is to safeguard one's work and ensure success. For if action does not harmonize with method performance does not harmonize with right,† and misfortune will overtake even those who are great and important. Therefore the sage uses method to tranquillize the people and right to govern them, ceremony‡ to stimulate them and benevolence to comfort them. And when these four qualities are practised the people are prosperous, and when they are neglected the people decline. Thus when Cheng Tang destroyed Jie the people of Xia rejoiced and were glad, and when Wu of Zhou destroyed Zhou (Xin) the people of Yin did not object. For what they did was in accordance with the will of heaven and of man, and so it was well done."§

toise hell or ox scapula bones and touched with a heated stylus. The heat caused the bone to crack and the answers to the question being divined were interpreted.

* The Way or *Dao* is a better translation where it appears in this paragraph. It is not just a procedural "method" as such, but rather, it is "the Way" and specifically the Confucian interpretation of it. "The Way" is achieved through the observance and practise of Confucian virtues.

† "Righteousness" is a better translation in this paragraph.

‡ The Confucian virtue of *li* or ritual propriety. This is the correct observance of rituals, in order to preserve civilization bring order and harmony to society.

§ Cheng Tang killed the tyrant Jie, last king of the Xia Dynasty and founded the Shang Dynasty. Wu destroyed Zhou Xin, last king of the Shang (or Yin) Dynasty, and founded the Zhou Dynasty.

Wu Qi describes the concordance of heaven and man, which is the loss of the Mandate of Heaven, or, in the European analogy, the "divine right." This concept of the Mandate of Heaven dates to the Zhou Dynasty, in the justification of the overthrow of the Shang by King Wu of Zhou. During the Warring States, the Confucian philosopher Mencius or Meng Zi (372–289 BCE) expanded on the concordance of the Mandate of Heaven and human will, in his concept of the "right to rebel." The concept of the "right to rebel" if

Chapter III

The Master Wu said: To govern a country or control an army there must be training through ceremony and stimulation through duty, so that a sense of shame is inculcated.* For where people feel shame, if to a greater extent they will fight and if to a lesser extent they will resist. And if you fight it is easy to win, but if you only resist it is difficult. And it is said, when the Empire is at war five victories are a misfortune, four are a nuisance, three make a leader, two make a king and one makes an Emperor, so those who have gained an Empire by many victories are few, but those who lost one in this way are many."†

Chapter IV

The Master Wu said: "In starting military operations there are five things to consider. First, striving after fame; second, striving after profit; third, intensifying feelings of hostility; fourth, stirring up internal disorder; and fifth, causing famine (among the enemy).

There are also five designations for soldiers.‡ First, good§ soldiers; second, stout soldiers; third, valiant¶ soldiers; fourth, disorderly ones, and fifth, rebellious ones. Those who forbid violence and assist in quelling disorder are called good soldiers.** Those who rely on numbers and attack are known as

---

the ruler had lost the Mandate of Heaven (by acting without the Confucian virtues such as benevolence, righteousness, rites, etc) became the fundamental principle of political change in China, well into the 20th Century. It remains the prevalent political concept in the Chinese world view.

* Translation: "To govern the state or order the army there must be instruction through ritual propriety and stimulation through righteousness so a sense of shame is incalculated." The correct Confucian order and conduct is critical in the maintenance of peace and order through harmonious governance. Conflict occurs only through the failure of governance and harmony.

† The notion of war being the least desirable option is a common theme in the three classical texts.

‡ "Soldiers" or "armies" may be a more accurate interpretation.

§ "Righteous."

¶ "Hard" or "firm" soldiers.

** Translation: "Those who suppress the violent and assist in quelling disorder are called good soldiers."

stout soldiers. Those who are actuated by ferocity and raise armies are called valiant soldiers. Those who cast away all ceremony in their greed for gain are called disorderly. And those who stir up trouble and agitate the people when the country is in confusion and the inhabitants are weary are called rebellious. To control these five kinds there is a method for each. The good must be controlled by ceremony,* the stout by humility, the valiant by words, the disorderly by cunning, and the rebellious by authority."

Chapter V

The Marquis Wu inquired, saying: "I wish to know the Way to rule soldiers and manage people so that the country can be stabilized." Wu Qi replied: "The renowned rulers of old always respected the ceremonial relations between lord and subject, honored the rule of superior and inferior and so gave security to all the officers and people. They gave them instruction according to the customary ways, and collected and selected good material and so were prepared without anxiety.

"In ancient times Duke Huan of Qi mustered fifty thousand warriors and thereby became the leader of the feudal states.† Duke Wen of Jin assembled forty thousand men and advanced boldly so that he captured the territory he aimed at. Duke Mu of Qin raised thirty thousand braves and with them subdued his enemies on every side. Therefore the lord of a powerful country will take an estimate of his people, and those who are bold and energetic he will collect and make into one company. Then those who rejoice in aggressive warfare and who use their strength with effect and thereby display their valor he will collect in one company. Those who can climb high and march far and are light-footed and can run fast he will form into one

---

* Translation: "The righteous must be controlled by ritual propriety..."

† Marquis Huan of Qi (Huan 685-643 BCE) was one of the Five Hegemons, the feudal lords who rose to hegemony over the fiefdoms or states of the Spring and Autumn Period with the decline of the central power of the (Eastern) Zhou court.

company. Princes and ministers who have lost their rank and office, but hope to show their merit to their superiors, he will make into one company, and those who have lost their strongholds and run away from their posts, but hope to wipe away their ill-fame, he will also collect in one company. And these five kinds of soldiers will form a keen and disciplined army. With three thousand of them you can raise a siege if you operate from within outwards, and destroy an enemy's fortress if you proceed from without inwards."*

Chapter VI

The Marquis Wu said: "I should like to know the Way to determine my order of battle so that it will be firm in defense and victorious in attack."

Wu Qi answered and said: These are things that have to be seen on the spot. They are not easily explained. If you employ the wise and put them on top while you keep the incapable below, your array will already be decided. If you keep the people secure in their farms and dwellings and are kindly in your management of them your defense will already be firm. If the peasants are all for their own lord and against the neighboring provinces the victory is already won."†

The Marquis Wu was once deliberating about state affairs and his ministers could not comprehend him. So he retired from the Court looking very pleased. Then Wu Qi came forward and said: "Prince Zhuang of Chu once deliberated on matters of state and his ministers could not comprehend it. So

---

* This passage reveals clearly the trend for professionalisation and specialization in the Spring and Autumn Period. The use and organisation of men into companies specialized and elite troops is a startlingly modern concept. This is reminiscent of special forces, parachute troops, and commandos in the present day. The use of "those who have lost their strongholds and run away from their posts, but hope to wipe away their ill-fame" is strongly reminiscent of the "punishment battalions" of the German Army of the Second World War.

† The continuing theme of internal domestic harmony being the foundation of state security. A harmonious society would be a loyal society and not willing to support the enemy forces in the internecine conflicts of this time.

he retired from the Court looking sad. Then the Minister Shen asked why the Prince looked sad and he said: 'I have heard it said that the world never lacks a sage and the country is never without a wise man. He who gets the former as a teacher becomes a Prince and he who gets the latter as a friend becomes a Leader. Now I am without ability and my ministers cannot attain to this position. Therefore the Chu state is in danger.' That is why the Prince of Chu looked sad, but you look pleased." The ministers were inwardly apprehensive and then the Marquis Wu looked ashamed.*

Section II—Estimating the Enemy
Chapter I

The Marquis Wu said to Wu Qi: "Just now Qin threatens us on the west and Chu encompasses us on the south. Zhao attacks us on the north, Qi approaches on the east, Yan cuts us off in the rear while Han comes up against our front. We have to defend ourselves against the armies of these six provinces on four sides, but our forces are inadequate. What then is to be done?"

Wu Qi replied: "The Way to make the country secure is to regard precaution as the most important thing. The lord who has already prepared can keep misfortune at a distance. The ministers should discuss the ways of the six countries. Now the Qi army is solid but not firm, the Qin forces are scattered but natural fighters, the Chu are concentrated but not enduring, the Yan army defends but cannot advance, and the men of the three Jin states are orderly but not effective.†

---

* This is a commentary on Confucian virtue. The Marquis Wu, in smiling at his intellectual superiority over his ministers, displays a lack of humility. It is also a dangerous situation when the ministers can not match the ruler intellectually, especially when the ruler admits his lack of ability.

† The Zhou dynasty state of Jin was partitioned into the states of Han, Wei, and Zhao in 403 BCE when the Viscounts Jing of Han, Wen of Wei, and Lie of Zhao forced the Zhou King Lie to elevate their rank to Marquis, thus marking the political independence of their respective states. This point is considered to mark the beginning of the Warring States period.

"The character of the Qi state is violent, its territory is wealthy and both the lord and his ministers are proud and luxurious, but stingy to the ordinary people, lax in rule and with incomes unequally distributed. So there are two parties in its army, the front solid but the rear unstable. Therefore it can be described as solid but not firm.

"The Way to attack him is to divide our forces into three parts and strike at him on the right and left. Thus threatening him, if you follow up the attack his army will he broken.

"The character of the Qin in state is strong and its country precipitous. Its rule is strict and reward and punishment just. The people are unyielding and have a pugnacious temper. So they may be described as scattered but natural fighters.

"The Way to attack them is to give them an advantage at first and then to retire. Their officers will wish to take it, and push on and become separated from their leader. Then you profit by this want of cohesion and attack the separate parts, and by ambushing troops at the right opportunity their commander may be captured.

"The Chu are by nature weak and their territory is extensive. Their government is confused and the people are exhausted. That is why they are called concentrated but not enduring.

"The Way to attack them is to make an onset and throw their camp into contusion. This will deprive them of spirit, and if you advance rapidly they will quickly retire. If then they are broken and tired out they will not fight and their forces will lose the battle.

"The character of Yan is circumspect and the people are respectful. They like courage and right and are clever at devising stratagems. So they defend but do not advance.

"To attack them approach and press on them, then break away and retire. Then if you quickly take them in the rear by surprise the officers will be in doubt and the men apprehensive. Then we can conceal our cavalry and chariots so as to evade their vigilance and capture their general.

"The three Jin states are in the middle country and their nature is peaceable. Their government is just and the people are tired of war. They are trained in warfare but despise their generals. Their revenues are small and their officers have no inclination to die. So they may be described as orderly but not effective.

"To attack them keep them at a distance but press on them, and when their men come against you do not engage them, but when they retire pursue them. Thus you can tire their army out. Such is their army.

"But in an army there will certainly be officers fierce as tigers, strong enough to lift a tripod* with ease, and swift of foot as wild horses, who will raise their banners and kill a general. And those who know their business will carefully select such men and set them aside and cherish and honor them, for they are the ones to command armies. If you use properly five such soldiers of strength and swiftness and resolution to destroy the enemy, you will surely obtain a decisive victory.

"The officers in a strong army are men who are attached to their parents and wives and children, and who are stimulated by rewards and fearful of punishment. They will endure long, and if a situation is clearly estimated they can attack twice their number."

"Very good," said Marquis Wu.

Chapter II

The Marquis Wu said: "In considering the enemy there are eight cases where you can fight with him without divination.† First, in a high wind and great cold, when the men get up early and move and cut the ice and cross the water and are not afraid of hardship. Second, in the height of summer when the heat is

---

* A "tripod" or *ding* is a large ritual bronze cauldron for cooking used in ancestral sacrifices, and seen as a measure of power and prestige.

† Divination has formed an essential part of Chinese life for millennia. The earliest known surviving Chinese scripts are passed down from the late Shang Dynasty period ca. 1300BCE, where divinations were recorded on tortoise shells and ox scapula bones. In this chapter however, Wu Qi suggests that the knowledge and intuition of these "sure bet" aspects of strategic advantage negates the need for divination.

excessive and they get up late and have no time left. They run fast and suffer from hunger and thirst and have to go a long distance. Third, when the army has been in the field a long time and there are no more provisions, and the peasants are enraged and many false rumors are started and the general cannot stop them. Fourth, when the army has its gear all worn out and there is no more fuel or fodder, while the weather is gloomy and rainy and they want to go foraging and cannot. Fifth, where the army is not large and is where there is little water so that men and horses are ill, and they cannot get assistance from their neighbors. Sixth, when they have a long way to go and the enemy is approaching and officers and men are tired and apprehensive. When they are worn out and have not yet eaten and have just taken off their buff-coats to rest. Seventh, when the general is negligible and the officers incompetent and both officers and men are not tough, so that the whole army is apt to take alarm. The general will flee and nobody will help them. Eighth, when they are in the field but not yet settled, and encamped but not yet prepared. When they are going up a slope or crossing a precipice, half concealed and half emerged. In all these cases you can attack without doubt.

"There are six cases where without divination you must avoid attacking.* First, where the enemy territory is very large, and the people numerous and wealthy. Second, where the upper classes love the lower and extend their favor widely among them. Third, where rewards are sure and penalties well considered, so that operations are correctly timed. Fourth, where the efficient are proclaimed and given precedence, and the wise are appointed and properly utilized. Fifth, when their army is very large and the soldiers well equipped. Sixth, when they have helpers on all sides and the assistance of a great country. Thus, if you are not equal to the enemy you must unquestionably avoid him. That is to say, you must understand the pos-

---

* Similarly, these are "sure bets" for failure and do not need divination—these conditions must be known as a truth.

sibilities before advancing, and realize the difficulties before retreating."*

Chapter III

The Marquis Wu inquired, saying: "I wish to determine which side will win by gaining knowledge of the internal state of the enemy by examining his external conditions, and to understand his halting by considering his advance. Can you tell me how to do so?"

Wu Qi replied: "If the enemy comes on moving aimlessly with his banners in uneasy disorder, and men and horses often turn and look backward, then you can attack with one-tenth of his force and be sure of throwing him into confusion.

"When the feudal lords have not assembled and lord and ministers do not yet know each other, when the moats and ramparts are not finished and the prohibition orders not yet published, the army corps will be in a state of upheaval so that if they wish to advance they cannot, and if they wish to retreat they do not dare. Then you can attack twice your numbers with half your forces, and risk a hundred fights without danger."

Chapter IV

The Marquis Wu inquired, saying: "What is really the best method of attacking an enemy?"

Wu Qi replied: "In handling troops one must consider the strong and weak points of the enemy and quickly decide where is the point of danger. When the enemy has come a long way and his formations are not yet ordered you may attack, and you may do likewise when he has had a meal but has not yet got into line again. When he has lost an opportunity and has not fol-

---

* The state that met these conditions would be an ideal Confucian state, ruled with virtue so that harmony and order created a state that could not be divided socially by rebellion and one which would be loyal to the ruler due to his wise and benevolent government. This is what Wu Qi advocates.

lowed up an advantage, attack. When he has gone a long march and some of his men are lagging behind and he has not rested, then attack. Attack also when he is crossing water and has only got half across. Attack too when he is on a steep or narrow path. When his standards are in disorder, when his columns are changing formation, or when the general is separated from his men and when their minds are apprehensive, then attack. And in such cases select the smartest men and send them in to charge, dividing the soldiers into parties and so making successive attacks. And attack suddenly and decisively."

Section III—On Controlling Soldiers
Chapter I

The Marquis Wu inquired, saying: "What is the first thing in training soldiers?"

Wu Qi replied: "The first thing to elucidate is the four lightnesses, the two heavinesses, and the one reliability."

"What are these?" said the Marquis.

And Wu Qi answered: "That the horses should be light on the ground, that the chariots should be light for the horses, that the men should be light in the chariots, and that the battle should be light for the men. If you know the rough and easy places then the horses will be light on the ground. If you have straw and fodder at the proper time then the chariots will be light for the horses. If you have plenty of straw and washers* then the men will be light in the chariots. If the spears are sharp and the buff-coats strong then the battle will be light for the men. If men advance the reward should be heavy and if they retreat the punishment should be heavy. And in the application of these there should be reliability. These are the things that when clearly considered and put into practise are the chief cause of victory."

---

* Translation: "If the axles are sufficiently greased…"

Chapter II

The Marquis Wu inquired, saying: "What is it that makes soldiers win victories?"

Wu Qi replied: "It is discipline* that makes them victorious."

The Marquis again asked, saying: "Does it not lie in their numbers?"

Wu Qi replied, saying: "If the regulations are not clear the rewards and penalties will not be reliable. They will not halt at the bell and they will not advance at the drum, so if you have a million of this sort what use will they be? What is meant by discipline is to have ceremony when at rest and stern menace when in action. So when they advance the enemy cannot withstand them and when they retire he cannot pursue. They move either forward or backward in correct order, and their right and left wings obey the signal banners. If they are cut off they keep their formation, and if they are scattered they move accordingly. And this whether they are secure or in dangerous places. An army like this can cooperate and cannot be divided. It can be maneuvered without becoming weary, and when it is launched at an objective the Empire cannot withstand it. It is what is called a father-and-son force."†

Chapter III

The Master Wu said: "When an army is on the march the order of advance or retreat must not be upset. Suitable supplies of food and drink must not be omitted, and the strength of men and horses must not be depleted. These three things must be

---

* "Control" is a better translation, taking in discipline, administration, and command. This can be used throughout the chapter. See also Fu (1985) p106 and Sawyer (1993) p459.

† This refers to the relationship between the commander or ruler and the army. It is an analogy to the father and son relationship, whereby in the Confucian system the virtues of benevolence, righteousness, loyalty, propriety, and filial piety act in harmony to produce a relationship where the father acts in leadership, the son in obedience, and where both father and son have clearly defined roles and responsibilities. In a harmonized father and son relationship, the family, and by analogy, the ruler/commander and army acts in unity.

carried out by obedience to the orders of superiors, for it is by such discipline that victory is produced.

"If there is no order in maneuvering and no proper supply of food and drink, horses and men will be wearied and will not know where to rest, so that they will not obey the orders of their superiors. And if these orders are disregarded disorder supervenes, and if they fight they will be defeated."

Chapter IV

The Master Wu said: "As to the field of battle it is the abiding-place of the dead. And he who decides to die will live, and he who wishes to live will die. And the good general is as one who sits in a leaky ship or lies under a burning house. He sees to it that the intelligence of the enemy does not fathom his plans, while their braves do not rival his in ferocity. So he can deceive the enemy. And it is said that the damage sustained in handling an army may well be greater than was anticipated. And the misfortunes of an army corps arise from suspicion."*

Chapter V

The Master Wu said: "People die because they are incapable and are defeated because they are unsuitable. Therefore the most important thing in handling troops is to train them. If one man is trained for war he can teach ten, if ten are trained they can instruct a hundred, a hundred can train a thousand, a thousand ten thousand and ten thousand an army corps (37,500).† Then we match short communications against long, ease against hardship and good feeding against hunger. When

---

* Translation: It may be better translated as "And the good general is as one who sits in a leaky ship or lies under a burning house. There is not enough time for the wise to plan, or for the courageous to get angry. One can only engage the enemy! The greatest harm in the use of arms is hesitation, the disasters that strike the Three Armies is born in doubt." Sadler has translated "the Three Armies" as "army corps."

† Sadler continues to use "the Three Armies" as "army corps," hence the figure of 37,500. A better translation is "and ten thousand men can train the Three Armies."

round you make your men square, when sitting you make them rise, when marching you make them halt, when going to the left you make them go to the right, when advancing you make them retire, when divided you bring them together, when in close formation you scatter them, so that they may learn every varying movement. Then they are given their weapons. This is what a general has to do."

Chapter VI

The Master Wu said: "In military instruction the rule is that short men should carry the long and short spears, and tall men the bow and crossbow. That the strong should carry the banners and the brave the bells and drums. The weaker should serve in the commissariat, and the cleverer should make the strategic plans. Men from the same villages should be brought together, and the squads of five and ten should protect each other. At one beat of the drum the men fall in. At two they drill in companies. At three they hasten to meals. At four they prepare for action. At five they get in marching order. When they hear the drums sound all together they know the banners will be raised."

Chapter VII

The Marquis Wu inquired, saying: "I suppose there is a Way for an army corps to advance and halt, is there not?"*

Wu Qi replied: "You must not come up against Heaven's cooking stove or the Dragon's head. The former means the mouth of a great valley and the latter the side of a great mountain. You must have the Blue Dragon on the right, the White Tiger on the left, the Red Bird in front, and the Dark Warrior behind.† The star Zhao Yao in the Dipper should be above you

---

* "The Three Armies."

† The four cardinal directions are represented by four celestial spirits, the constellations known as the Blue Dragon for the east, the White Tiger in the west, the Red Bird in

and beneath it you should carry on.* And when you fight be very careful to watch the quarter from which the wind blows. If it is behind you then call up your men and follow it, but if it is against you take up a strong position and wait."

Chapter VIII

The Marquis Wu inquired, saying: "I suppose there is a proper way for the soldiers to feed their horses, is there not?"

Wu Qi replied: "Yes, horses should always be treated so that they are comfortable, and given suitable food and drink so regulated that they are not over or under fed. In winter their stables should be kept warm and in summer shaded and cool. Their hair and mane should be cut, and their four hoofs carefully trimmed. Their eyes and ears should be controlled so that they may not be startled, and they should be taught to gallop and pursue. They should be trained to be quiet in their movements, and they are most effective where there is mutual affection between man and horse.

"The furniture of the chariot and horse comprises saddle, bridle, bit, and reins, and they must be kept strong and in order. Horses do not get damaged at the end but at the beginning. They are not harmed by too little food but by too much. Toward dusk on a long journey the men must dismount many times. For though this may tire the men, it is more important not to tire the horses. They should be kept with some strength in reserve. We have to prepare against the enemy overthrowing us. Those who understand this clearly will be able to bestride the whole Empire."

---

the south, the Dark Warrior in the north.
* The star *Zhao Yao* represents the center of the cardinal points. Thus Wu Qi teaches "command from the center."

Section IV—Argument about Generals
Chapter I

The Master Wu said: "He must have both civil and military qualities who is a commander of armies. For dealing with soldiers needs both strength and gentleness. Now those who discuss generals always think of their valor. But valor is only one of the many qualities of a general, and the valorous type of general is apt to join battle lightly and carelessly, without knowing how to profit by it, so that he cannot win.

"There are therefore five things that a general must consider important. First, principle; second, preparation; third, results; fourth, caution; fifth, economy. Principle means controlling the many as one man. Preparation means going out of your own gate as though about to meet an enemy. Result means not clinging to life when you face the foe. Caution means behaving after victory as though the battle was only just beginning. Economy means being sparing of regulations so as not to cause irritation. The proper conduct for a general is not to linger at home when he receives his orders, but to order the return when he has beaten the enemy. So when the army marches out he has the glory of death and not the shame of living."

Chapter II

The Master Wu said: "In military affairs there are four opportunities.* First, the opportunity of spirit;† second, that of geography; third, that of circumstances; and fourth, that of power. When the men of an army corps,‡ an army of a million men, are influenced in their feelings entirely by one man, it is what is called the opportunity of spirit. When the path is narrow and the way steep and so makes a great stronghold where

---

* Opportunities to create strategic advantage.

† *Qi* or chi the internal energy. Here Sadler uses "spirit," to convey a meaning to *qi* that may also mean "morale" or "fighting spirit."

‡ "The Three Armies."

ten men can hold a thousand at bay, it is what is called the opportunity of geography. When by good management in using spies and sending light troops the enemy's forces are scattered and their loyalty to their superiors undermined, so that high and low are mutually hostile, this is called the opportunity of circumstances. When the naves and linen-pins of the chariots are tight, and the oars and rudders of the ships well fitted, the officers well trained for battle, and the horses broken to the right pace, it is what is called the opportunity of power. He who understands these four things will make a general.

"So the virtues of dignity, justice, kindness, and courage are the things that suffice in leading subordinates and giving security to the people.* By them awe and doubt are imposed on an enemy. When orders are given inferiors do not dare to disobey, and where these qualities are bandits† do not venture to oppose. Where they exist the country is strong, and where they are absent it is ruined. And one who has them is a good general."

Chapter III

The Master Wu said: "Drums and gongs stimulate the ear, and flags and banners stimulate the eye, as prohibitions and penalties stimulate the mind. If the ear is stimulated by sound it must be purified, and if the eye is stimulated by color it must be clarified, so if the mind is stimulated by punishment it will be disciplined. If there is a country without these three things it will certainly be defeated by an enemy. So it is said that the men must always follow where the general leads, and must advance even to the death where the general orders."

Chapter IV

The Master Wu said: "What is needed in war is to obtain the

---

* Translation: "His reputation, virtue, benevolence, and courage must be sufficient in leading subordinates and giving security to the people."

† "The enemy."

name of the enemy leader and decide on his capacity, so as to calculate what his plans will be, and make use of this survey to obtain success without great difficulty. If this general is a fool and relies on others you can deceive him and lure him on. If he is greedy and careless of reputation you can use bribes to buy him. If his movements are unimportant and he has no plans you can tire him out, and embarrass him. If the superiors are wealthy and proud and the inferiors poor and resentful, you can divide them and use spies. If they are full of hesitation as to whether to advance or retire and their men have no confidence, they can be shaken and put to flight. If the officers despise their commander and are inclined to go back home, so that they defend easy places and give up difficult ones, you can oppose them and take them. If your position is one from which it is easy to advance and difficult to retire then get the enemy to advance, but if it is one where advance is difficult and retreat easy then press on him and attack. If your army is on wet ground, lead it where there is no water, for if there should be long continued rain the ground will be flooded and you may sink. If your army is on rough swampy ground where the grass and thorns are deep and thick, if the wind blows strongly you can set it alight and destroy it. If they stay long in one place both officers and men become indolent, so that the whole army is unprepared and can be taken by surprise and attacked."

Chapter V

The Marquis Wu inquired, saying: "Suppose two armies are facing each other and we do not know about the other general, what tricks do we use if we wish to find out about him?"

Wu Qi replied: "You take some low but brave fellows and lead out a party of them light-armed to try the enemy by flight. They are not to be deployed to get any advantage, but to see how the enemy will come on. If his deportment and movements are all orderly, and when pursuing us in our flight he is wary and does not overtake us, and when an advantage presents itself he is cunning and does not appear to perceive it, then you may know that the general is a wise one and that it is better not to attack.

"But if his men are noisy and clamorous and his banners confused, while the soldiers run hither and thither without orders, some going this way and some that. When we flee they pursue but are afraid to approach, and when they see an advantage they are afraid to take it. This shows a foolish general, and though his forces are superior you can gain the victory over them."

Section V—On Sudden Emergency
Chapter I

The Marquis Wu inquired, saying: "If the chariots are strong and the horses good and the general brave and the men bold, and you come on the enemy suddenly and fall into confusion and lose formation, what is to be done then?"

Wu Qi replied: The rule of battle is that in the daytime order is kept by flags and banners and at night by bells and drums and fifes. If the signal flag points to the left they go to the left, and if the right then to the right. When also the drum beats the advance they go forward, and when the bell sounds they halt. If the fife goes once it means advance and if twice it means assemble. Those who do not obey these orders are punished. If the whole army corps is thus under authority, and the officers and men obey orders, no enemy is too strong to fight and no army is too powerful to attack."*

Chapter II

The Marquis Wu inquired, saying: "When the enemy is many and we are few, what do we do?"

---

* This is the emphasis on training and instant reaction to training to overcome surprise. This is the equivalent to repetitive training in "contact drills" of the modern soldier.

Wu Qi replied: "If the ground is flat and open avoid him, but if it is narrow withstand him, as it is said, for one to attack ten nothing is as good as a narrow place and for ten to attack a hundred nothing is as good as a steep one, while for a thousand to attack ten thousand nothing is as good as a ravine. For if you take a few men and make a sudden surprise attack on a narrow road with a loud sounding of gongs and drums, the biggest army may be thrown into confusion. So it is said that a big army should be maneuvered in open ground, but a small one in a narrow place."

Chapter III

The Marquis Wu inquired, saying: "Suppose an army is large and disciplined and also brave, with high ground behind it and far from any steep place, with a hill on the right and water on the left, protected by deep moats and high ramparts and defended by powerful archery. When it retires it is like a moving mountain and when it advances it is like a blizzard, while it is also supplied with provisions in plenty. It is therefore difficult to hold out long against it and what then are we to do?"

Wu Qi replied: "A big question indeed! This is not a matter of chariots and horsemen but of the strategy of a sage. One must have a thousand chariots and ten thousand horsemen, with infantry as well, and they must be divided into five armies. Each army must be on a road so that if there are five armies on five different roads the enemy will certainly be perplexed, for he will not know where they will operate. If the enemy stands on the defensive and keeps his men in their strongholds, then we send spies quickly to see what his plans are. If he listens to their proposals he may acquiesce and retire, but if he does not he will kill the envoys and burn their letters. Then our five armies will join battle, and if they win they will not follow it up (for fear of ambush), but if they do not they will get away quickly. As though making a pretended flight they will go easily and fight suddenly. One army will close in on his front and another will cut him off behind, and both will attack with gags in their mouths (so that they keep silent). Either on the left or on the right the attack will be at the weakest place and the five armies will come together so that they will be sure to gain the advantage. This is the Way to attack a stronger force."

Chapter IV

The Marquis Wu inquired, saying: "If the enemy is near at hand and is about to attack and we wish to retire and there is no road, so that the men are therefore in a panic, what is to be done?"

Wu Qi replied: "This is the device I should use. If we are superior in numbers we can divide and take advantage of it, but if we are inferior we must find some way to come to terms with them. And thus complying, but not giving up the war, even a great force can be overcome."

Chapter V

The Marquis Wu inquired, saying: "If we meet the enemy in a valley and the sides are very steep, and his force is superior to ours, how about it?"

Wu Qi replied: "In meeting with all kinds of hills and wooded valleys, great mountain ranges and marshes, you must traverse them rapidly and get away from them quickly. So do not get led into them. If you suddenly meet an enemy on a height or in a valley then be the first to sound the drum vigorously and attack, shooting with your archery and crossbows. And so shooting some and making some prisoners you will see if he is likely to fall into disorder, when you can push your attack with success."

Chapter VI

The Marquis Wu inquired, saying: "If we meet an enemy where there are lofty mountains on right and left and the ground is so very narrow that we cannot venture to attack, what is to be done?"*

Wu Qi replied: "That is what is called a valley battle. Here superior numbers are no use. We must get together the cleverest officers and engage the enemy, making the advance with light and efficient troops. The chariots must be grouped and the cavalry ranged in support, and ambushes made on all sides. They should be many miles apart, and the troops should not be visible. Meanwhile the enemy will be well entrenched and will not venture to move. Then our forces will raise their banners and advance in order outside the mountains and take station there. This will make the enemy apprehensive, and our chariots and cavalry will threaten him and allow him no rest. This is the manner of a valley battle."

Chapter VII

The Marquis Wu inquired, saying: "Suppose we are engaging the enemy and come on a great watery swamp. The chariot wheels collapse and the poles are submerged as the floods bear down on the chariots and horsemen, and as we have no boats we can go neither forward nor backward. What would you do then?"

Wu Qi replied: "This is what is called a water battle. Chariots and horsemen are no use. You must halt for a while, get up on a high place and survey the situation. Then you can see how the water lies, whether it is extensive and what is its depth, so that you can find some device to get the victory. If the enemy goes to cross this water, attack him when he is half across."

Chapter VIII

The Marquis Wu inquired, saying: "If there is long continued rain so that the horses fall and the chariots stick, and you are

---

* Translation: "...we cannot venture to attack, nor retreat, what is to be done?"

attacked by the enemy on all sides so that the whole army is uneasy and panicky, what do you propose to do then?"

Wu Qi replied: "While the sky looks dark and rainy I would stay still, but when it brightens then I would move. Choose the high ground and avoid the low, and hurry on your heavy chariots. This is the method to follow whether you either halt or move. If the enemy moves too be sure to hang on to his rear."

Chapter IX

The Marquis Wu inquired, saying: "If bandits* make a sudden raid and seize our rice-fields and lands and take our horses and cattle, what is then to be done?"

Wu Qi replied: "When bandits come remember that they are strongest[†] then and so be on the defensive and do not meet them. But when they begin to draw off at dusk they will be encumbered with their stuff and there will be apprehension in their minds. They will retire hurriedly and there will certainly be stragglers. That is the time to follow them up and attack, and then their force can be overthrown."

Chapter X

The Master Wu said: "As to the Way to attack an enemy and surround his stronghold. When his strong places have been reduced his mansion will be entered, his revenues taken, and his goods confiscated.[‡] But his trees must not be cut down nor his

---

* Raiding force or foraging force.

† Translation: "When the raiders come, consider their strength..." After Fu (1985) p166.

‡ Sadler's translation is erroneous to the point of changing the meaning of Wu Qi.

Translation: "When his fortifications have been reduced, enter his palaces of public administration, take control of his bureaucrats, and use his systems of administration." After Fu (1985) p166. Wu Qi implies that the objective in warfare is not destruction, but rather a method of statecraft with the ultimate objective of implementing control and order over society. A virtuous ruler that goes to war with righteous justification does not therefore aim to annihilate the enemy and reduce his state. Rather, having defeated the enemy, he acts with benevolence and restores his order and administration. Contrast the success of the Allied occupation of Japan from 1945 when the majority of the Japanese administrative and government systems remained intact, with debacle of the occupation

houses sold, nor his millet crops taken, nor his animals killed, nor his grain-stores burnt. You must show no brutality to the people,* and if they wish to surrender you must allow them and let them dwell secure."

Section VI—On the Encouragement of Officers
Chapter I

The Marquis Wu inquired, saying: "Is severe punishment and just reward sufficient to ensure victory?"

Wu Qi replied: "I do not think severity and justice exhaust all the possibilities for a minister. They are good, but cannot entirely be relied on. That the men should obey willingly when orders are issued and commands given. That they fight willingly when they meet the foe. And that they die willingly when they exchange blows. These three conditions are those on which the greatest reliance is to be placed."

The Marquis Wu said: "And how can this be brought about?"

The reply was: "When the lord singles out the capable and promotes them and entertains them, and when he stimulates those who lack capacity."

Whereupon the Marquis Wu made a reception in his palace and entertained his officers and high officials in three divisions. The most meritorious sat in the front division and were served with a banquet in the finest vessels, and with the sacrificial animals. Those next in merit sat in the middle division and were served with a banquet, but in somewhat inferior vessels, while those of no merit sat behind and were served with a banquet in vessels not at all valuable. When the entertainment was over they went out, and outside the palace gate a distribution of presents was made to the fathers and mothers, wives and children of the meritorious, in which the same discrimination was made. And to the houses of those who had died envoys were sent every

of Iraq in 2002, when the Baathist system of administration and government was systematically dismantled, thus contributing to plunging society into internecine chaos.

* Translation: You must show the people that you hold no vicious intentions..."

year to make presents to their parents in recognition of their services, and to show that they were still held in remembrance.

After this had gone on for three years the Qin people raised an army and advanced to the west river. When the Wei officers heard of this, without waiting for the orders of their superiors they put on their armor and fought against them. And there were tens of thousands of them.

Then the Marquis Wu called Wu Qi and said: "This is the result of what you previously taught me."

Wu Qi replied: "I have heard that all men have their strong and weak points, and their times of courage and depression. If you send forth fifty thousand incapable men* as an experiment and let me lead them against the enemy, if I fail and do not win we shall be a laughing-stock to the neighboring lords and lose all our prestige in the Empire.† Now consider a desperate bandit who is lying in ambush in wild country, and is pursued by a thousand men. He must be looked on as an owl or a tiger, and they will be afraid of his suddenly springing out and injuring them. So that one man who will risk his life can terrify a thousand. If I have fifty thousand men and meet one of these desperate bandits, if I lead them to the attack he will be difficult to oppose."

So the Marquis Wu followed this advice and took five hundred chariots and three thousand horsemen, with which he defeated the Qin force of five hundred thousand. Such is the efficacy of the encouragement of officers.

One day before the battle Wu Qi gave his orders to the whole army, saying: "All officers must follow my orders when they meet the enemy's chariots, horse, and foot. Chariots must take enemy chariots, horsemen horsemen, and footmen footmen, or they will not be considered efficient even if they break through the enemy's forces. If this order is executed without confusion your might will shake the whole Empire."

---

* Translation: "Previously undistinguished men."
† Better translated as "throughout the world."

NOTES

Sun Tzu

Chapter II, page 95: Chariots.—The chariot of four horses and three armored men, the captain, his armor-bearer, and the driver, was the prominent unit of the Chinese army. Each chariot was supported by 25 foot-soldiers and followed by 72 light armed men. Its axles and pole were covered with leather and it was plated with bronze, this being replaced by iron under the Leader Duke Huan of Qi in the 7th century B.C. The battalion should be composed of 500 men, the regiment of 2,500, and the army or division of 15,000, but these numbers varied. The infantry were conscripted peasants who resented this duty. Cavalry were not used by the Chinese till the 4th century, when they were introduced by the Tartarized King Wuling of Zhao, 329-299 B.C.*

Chapter IX, page 109: Huangdi.—The Yellow Emperor, ascribed to 2698 B.C., the earliest period of Chinese history.

Chapter XIII, page 121: Yin, also called Shang, dynasty 1766-1154 B.C. Xia dynasty 2205-1818 B.C. Zhou dynasty, 1122-225 B.C.

Sima Rangju

Chapter I, page 131.—The men of old refers to the Ancient Sovereigns Yao and Shun of the golden age before the Xia dynasty, when all was simplicity and righteousness under a paternal ruler who set the example.

---

* King Wuling of Zhao's military reform of "barbarian uniforms and cavalry" reform introduced cavalry and battle uniforms modelled on those of nomadic barbarian tribes such as the Huns. Sima Qian, "Zhao Ce Jia" *Shiji*. ("House Of Zhao," *The Records of the Grand Historian*), vol 43. 109 BC to 91 BC. Zhonghua Publishing House, Beijing 1959.

Page 133.—Yu of Xia, Tang of Yin and Wu of Zhou were the founders of these dynasties.

Wu Qi

Section I, Chapter V, page 167: Huan of Qi.—The first Leader of the feudal lords of the Zhou dynasty, 685-643 B.C.

Section III, Chapter VII, page 177: The Blue Dragon, etc.—These are the "Four Quadrants": Blue Dragon, East; White Tiger, West; Red Bird, South; Dark Warrior, North.